YOUR BRAIN SWINGS EVERY CLUB

Chasing 10 Hz

by

Dr. Izzy Justice

With Foreword by **Brad Faxon**
&
Epilogue by **Jim Hinckley**

YOUR BRAIN SWINGS EVERY CLUB

Chasing 10 Hz

Disclaimer:
This book is for informational purposes only and is not intended as medical advice. The author and publisher disclaim any liability for any adverse effects resulting directly or indirectly from the use or application of the contents of this book. Readers should consult qualified health professionals for advice on any medical concerns.

Online Resources Notice:
Every effort has been made to ensure that web links and online resources referenced in this book are accurate and active at the time of publication. However, websites and their contents may change over time. The author and publisher are not responsible for the availability, accuracy, or content of these external resources.

ISBN: 979-8-9985212-2-5

For inquiries, contact: www.neuro580.com or Amazon

Printed in the United States by Amazon

"As a coach, I'm constantly looking for new ways to help my clients and asking: How can we help athletes become more aware, more adaptable, and more consistent under pressure? Dr. Izzy Justice's work has been extremely helpful in answering that question and the strategies he teaches and the tools he gives have helped me become a better coach. This book is a guide to understanding that your swing isn't just a movement—it's a neurological event. When you begin to train the brain as intentionally as you train the body, everything starts to change. I truly believe that Izzy's work and this book will help improve anybody's game and could be the breakthrough you need to play your best golf when it matters the most to you."

—**Chris Como, Instructor**

"In competition, I was always quick to blame technique when something went wrong. Thanks to my time with Dr. Justice, I now realize that a poor shot is oftentimes a product of having high brain frequency, leading to a distracting thought or a lousy target. The use of neurohacks has given me the ability to slow down, lower my brain frequency, and dominate my last thoughts before I pull the trigger, no matter the circumstances. Give yourself the best opportunity to succeed by 'getting to green' with Dr. Justice."

—**Cole Hammer, KFT Tour Player**

"Dr. Justice's insights into how the brain works could transform how we approach golf—technically and mentally. Understanding the brain's role in the game can help players, coaches, and parents better tackle its challenges."

—**Nick Hardy, PGA Tour Player**

"This quote by Dr. Izzy Justice marvelously encapsulates the message of this eye-opening book: 'Your best shot and your worst shot are rarely separated by physical ability or technique, and almost entirely by the crowd noise in your brain over those shots.' Izzy has the uncanny ability to take complex mental concepts and make them easy to comprehend, and more importantly, easy to apply. Entertaining, enlightening and easy to read, this book is a must-have for any aspirant golfer."

—**Mark Immelman, Sports Broadcaster, Instructor**

"The term neuroscience can be a daunting subject to most people, but with this book it no longer is. Dr Izzy does an amazing job of giving practical tools to understand how our brain works, and how this can directly and immediately improve performance both on the course and off the course. This is a must read!"

—**Phil Knowles, PGA Tour**

"This book is an enlightened journey for golf and life. For years I always played my best when I was happy, calm, and in the moment. I knew that meditation, routine and unwavering belief always helped me play my best, but I didn't know why. Dr Justice quantifies the why. It's all about keeping the electricity low in your brain. He explains how you can use neurohacks to decrease the electricity so you can pick a great target and hold it through the swing. Anytime, anywhere, and any situation - you can use these techniques to be your best."

—**Scott McCarron, Champions Tour Player**

"The book you are about to read by Dr. Izzy Justice has the potential to change not only your game but your relationship to golf forever. You will finally understand the role your brain plays in determining the outcome of EVERY shot. Without the wisdom contained in these pages you will stay lost looking for the answers to your golfing issues in the wrong place."

—**Karl Morris, Golf Performance Coach, MindFactor**

"The work Dr. Justice is doing reminds me of things I did well when I played well. Now there's neuroscience behind it! This should be fully integrated into Golf permanently!"

—**Hall Sutton, PGA & 2-Time Players Champion**

"I truly believe that success in the game of golf comes from attitude, self-belief, and investment into the constant process of improvement. Dr. Justice has provided me with knowledge of how my brain works and has helped me develop a weekly blueprint to revamp my process in a way that best fits my brain - how I think. Both in person and through this book, he has afforded me a refreshing take on the game that has helped propel me to both enjoy the game more on and off the course and win on one of the highest levels of the professional game. I strongly recommend this book for all types of golfers!

PS: I think you will be surprised how much Dr. Justice's teaching help on the course, in the conference room, and most importantly, at home! AIM HIGH!"

—**Kyle Westmoreland, KFT Tour Player**

DEDICATION

To Gary Mason, Coco, and Ami Jaan.

ACKNOWLEDGEMENTS

I love collaborative work. When minds come together for the healthy exploration of knowledge to improve the human condition, good things always happen.

I am grateful for the spirit of collaboration from: Marina Bobeldijk, Chris Como, Darcy Dhillon, Brad Faxon, Dino Ferrer, Cole Hammer, Nick Hardy, Jim Hinkley, Mark Immelman, Phil Knowles, Scott McCarron, Jim McClean, Jennifer Meller, Karl Morris, Salimah Mussani, Carla Overhiser, Tim Sheredy, Jeff Smith, Hal Sutton, Justin Tang, and Kyle Westmoreland. Sincere thanks also to my editor, Anjum Khan.

TABLE OF CONTENTS

FOREWORD

When I was a young boy growing up in the town of Barrington, Rhode Island, my Dad introduced me to the game of golf. I was maybe five or six years old. He was a scratch golfer, club champ and darn good athlete. He played college hockey at Norwich University in Vermont and introduced me to all kinds of sports as a kid. It was an ideal place to be raised, as we had the best in state public schools, better community and best of all, a Donald Ross golf course called Rhode Island Country Club.

My Dad, only 21 years senior, served as a Lieutenant in the US Army and instilled a strong work ethic in me at an early age. At 12 years of age, I signed up to be a caddie at RICC, and honestly, was naive about what would be instilled into me the next few summer seasons. The caddie master, Ralph Gunn, seemed to have a military background in the way he mentored and reminded us that the more we worked, the more we made and the more chances we had of moving up the caddie ranking list. The three Desisto brothers, Mike, Mark and Anthony, were dominant in the caddie rankings and scored more points, made more money and carried more loops than anyone else. It was apparent they were the barometer for excellence, and they were requested more often by the better member players. After seeing how diligent they were, they became mentors to me, stating you have to show the players how much you care about their game and help them in any way possible.

As a budding young player, one of the benefits of caddying was getting to play at Rhode Island Country Club on Mondays, and the occasional weekday afternoon. The Donald Ross course, right by Narragansett Bay, had some of the most beautiful and undulating greens. As my caddie experience grew, I was gaining the reputation of being an excellent greens reader. And often getting requested by the better players at the club. When these members would play early on Saturday and Sunday mornings, the morning dew on the green often left a track the ball would leave after being struck by the members' putter. It was amazing to watch a ball roll on greens with moisture, see the path the ball took, and how much the balls would break, especially at the end of the putt as the ball slowed down.

The thousands of putts I saw each summer season left an indelible mark in my mind of the starting line, the apex of the putt and the target or the hole. Ever since I qualified for the PGA Tour back in 1983, at the age of 22, I had the ability to capture a target on the greens. The images were vivid and captivating, something I could hold in my mind for what seemed like an eternity.

I first met Dr. Izzy Justice, through a longtime friend and fellow PGA Tour player, Scott McCarron. Scott and I always liked to discuss anyway possible to improve and Scott's first message about Izzy left me curious. In this book, *Your Brain Swings the Club*, Izzy explains how the brain works to best capture a target and reminds us that golf may be the only sport where we don't necessarily look at the target when we swing. Think bowling, free throw shooting, target practice, and how it's easy to look at the target while in motion. Izzy takes you through the process of how your mind works, how to best capture a target, and then put a process together that is simple and repeatable.

We have all experienced a great practice round, a flawless evening session on the range and an excellent performance on the course during a club match. But where is the consistency! Why does it seem so hard to repeat? And how can I keep missing those same short putts when they matter the most!? The answers are in these pages. Particularly exciting is the chapter on Putting, and the reminders of how picking out a vivid target, close to the hole, that you can hold in your mind is the only way to putt. And, you will learn the terminology and the process, not the routine, that you need to use in order to achieve more consistency and hole that putt time after time.

This book is interesting, and incredibly useful to help you get to the range and have a plan so that you will hit more good shots, hole more important putts, and most importantly, shoot lower scores.

Brad Faxon

Tour Player, Instructor, Broadcaster

01 | INTRODUCTION

My Journey to Neuroscience

Your best shot and your worst shot are rarely separated by physical ability or technique, and almost entirely by the crowd noise in your brain over those shots.

I have authored two previous books on Golf: *Golf EQ* and *GYRA Golf*. With this book, my goal is to continue to build on the body of knowledge based on three dominating sources:

1. Over 18K EEG brain scans on golfers that I had conducted (as of this publication) while they were hitting shots, mostly putting and short game.
2. Tacit knowledge and experience having worked with dozens of professional golfers from all over the world - high level amateurs, juniors, and a few recreational golfers.
3. Advancement of research in neuroscience on both the brain itself as well as its role in neuromuscular performance.

My academic background has entailed an unintended yet somewhat circuitous journey into Neuroscience over the past decade.

My initial college degree was a Bachelor of Science in Physics from Davidson College. The study of matter, forces, and electricity was at the core of understanding much of our human experience. I then went to acquire another Bachelor of Science in Civil Engineering from NC State University. A deeper understanding of structure, pressure, and forces led to understanding how to design bridges, roads, and systems carrying water. A great deal of an understanding of nature (topography, weather, etc.) and its forces was leveraged into my way of thinking and making sense of life.

For personal reasons, from my childhood growing up in Africa, my fascination shifted from a deep understanding of matter and nature to a deep understanding of human performance. I knew what it took to design the curvature of a road for cars traveling at a certain speed, for example, but what I found infinitely more fascinating was what it took to get people to perform at a high level. What systems and 'structures' would need to be in place in a company to make all the people run smoothly. I pivoted and got an MBA, followed by a Doctorate in Management, all the while working in Consulting firms on projects and in companies around the world, coaching clients and implementing high performance systems to support collaborative cultures for high performance. Even though I was good at this, something was missing from all the knowledge I had learned and experienced. I did not know what it was except that at the center of everything was a single human being.

It was not until I was exposed to the seminal work by Peter Salovey and John Mayer in their article "Emotional Intelligence", published in the journal *Imagination, Cognition, and Personality* that I found the missing element. For the first time, similar to the way I studied Physics and Engineering, I was exposed to what was 'under the hood' of the human experience. Having observed the workplace for over 20 years, I noticed that regardless of an individual's skills, if their emotional temperature was high, their skills eroded quickly, and performance suffered. I went on to author or co-author three books leveraging this framework: *Triathlete EQ, Golf EQ,* and *Healthcare EQ.* I thought I had it all figured and demystified the human rubric for performance until I asked the questions: *Where do thoughts and emotions come from? How are they created? Is there a way to go upstream of the human experience—where it all starts—and address things there so downstream work is easier?*

These questions peaked around 2015, and in 2016—about a decade after earning my Doctorate—I made yet another pivot ... into Neuroscience. Because I already had my Doctorate, for the first time I felt free to study a body of knowledge with freedom to go anywhere, to anyone, from any source, and learn it not for a grade on a paper or Certificate, but purely to understand it. This is what led to studying the upstream elements of the human experience, including performing under stress.

The analogy I want you to have as you read this book is to imagine that you have a beautiful cabin by a small river in the mountains. Every morning, you wake up and go out to your deck overlooking the river with your beverage of choice and enjoy the spectacular sunrise and sounds of water flowing. However, each morning a bag of trash from somewhere upstream comes down river and gets stuck right in front of your cabin. No problem. You go down there, pick up the bag and put it in your trash can. You then enjoy the rest of your day. There was a problem in your experience, and you solved it. But isn't the better solution to go upstream, see where it is coming from and stop it there? Sure, I think most of you would agree.

The human brain is that upstream source where everything comes from. Our feelings, thoughts, behaviors, and desired actions are all being manufactured in the brain and showing up to our awareness (conscious) only when they are downstream.

I suddenly found myself disappointed and almost angry that I had spent so much of my time, formally and experientially, trying to decode human performance and no one had ever guided me to study the brain's role. So much of my work was addressing and fixing downstream issues. So, you can imagine my surprise when, during a lecture I was attending (by Dr. Bing Brunton from the University of Washington), I came across words that would change the course of my life: Electricity is the Language of the Brain.

Wait, what? Electricity? The same electricity I studied in the 1980s at Davidson College? Electricity is the language of motor pattern and sequence to generate desired neuromuscular vector (direction and magnitude) forces. Wait, what? The same vector forces I learned and applied from Physics and Engineering? Electricity is used by one neuron to communicate to another carrying Action Potentials – the eventual outcome of thoughts, feelings, behavior – including desired motor function (like hitting a putt). Electricity.

But why electricity? Why not gravity or light or a form of internal pressure system like the cardiovascular system? Why must the language of the brain (and thereby memory and motor function) be electricity? Well, the answer is a lot simpler than the question.

If there is a bug that stings you behind your right shoulder, you need to know this immediately. Information about the nature of the sting needs to travel super-fast from that specific spot behind your shoulder to your brain and be processed as a threat. Memories have to be accessed quickly to give it a threat assessment. Any delay in this relay of travel of information could lead to the bug continuing to sting you. Within milliseconds, this relay is accomplished and your left hand and arm quickly, without any conscious thought, reach to the exact geospatial location of the bug bite and slap it away. This speed is necessary for this level of self-preservation, and only electricity can facilitate this kind of absolutely stunning speed of diagnostics and protection.

In addition to speed, imagine the lived human experience without movement. We all must move our heads to see something, use our arms and hands to grab something and feed ourselves, use our legs and feet for balance and walking or running to get food or run away from danger. This movement requires muscles to work together in some sequence and at some required level of speed. The language of motor movement has to be electricity—it could not possibly be anything else that we know of.

Wait again. I knew we could measure electricity and forces, but could we measure electricity in the brain? Yes, and we have been doing it successfully since about the 1920s. That is only about 100 years. I began to explore technologies to measure electricity (in the brain), and it turned out that most measurements were being done in either hospitals or research centers, and almost all were in the clinical setting. That means most of our research and knowledge of the brain is based on clinical conditions—where something is very wrong. This makes sense. It makes sense to study Alzheimer's, Dementia, Parkinsons, Schizophrenia, Huntington's Disease, TBI, and such. Studying these clinical conditions means we can find cures for them. The brain is incredibly complex and understanding neurobiology, neurochemistry, neuroanatomy, and neuro-electricity are all required for these clinical conditions. This understanding has led to the development of drugs and therapies that help many people suffering from these awful diseases.

My own mother died in 2022 from Alzheimer's. This is a type of disease that, in my view, is the worst of all. Who are we without any memory? Where did all her memories go and why could Mom not recognize me, her own son? What was happening in her brain? Trying to understand this in the ten or so years prior to her death pushed me with relentless motivation to study neuroscience not just from a human performance perspective, but also a deeply personal one.

I am not qualified to study these clinical conditions or cures, nor did I have resources to do so. I leave that for people far smarter than me. But I wanted to carve out a piece of this puzzle that perhaps clinical research was not inclined to address. So, I put everything into this new career pivot and focused on studying what I could.

There was one more personal motivation. My son was in High School Class of 2024 and a junior golfer with aspirations to play golf in college. From about 2014-2024, I took him to countless junior golf tournaments and went through all the ups and downs that any parent of a junior athlete can relate to. My son was aware of what I did for a living, working with professional athletes who would fly in and stay at our home. Even though I had perhaps a little higher 'street cred' because of my work, I was still his Dad, and he was still my son. I could not teach him what I was teaching Tour Players, not in style or content. With children, timing of the lesson is critical, not just the lesson. I forced myself to learn as much as I could about the neuroscience of performance because that gave me a much bigger basket of ideas to then pull from to coach him both as a child and as my child. I had to speak his language, which often meant being more creative and situational, as opposed to logical and formal.

My intense motivation to study the brain was driven by a combination of my job, the pain of my Mom's condition, and raising a junior golfer.

I was interested in knowing what is happening in a normal brain (not clinical) for far simpler measurable cognitive and neuromuscular performance goals, like when a golfer makes a putt or misses one. I was interested in knowing what the state of the brain is when one is calm and focused and making putts versus agitated and angry and missing putts. I was already working with coaches/athletes in all sports but leveraging Emotional Intelligence (EQ) Tools not neuroscience. I was not looking at the electricity in their brains. I did not know I could even do that.

There are many ways and equipment used to measure brain activity. The most common one is Magnetic Resonance Imaging (MRI) that uses a magnetic field and radio waves. This is possibly the most accurate way, but the equipment used is a massive machine requiring individuals to lay horizontal and very still. This is great for clinical purposes, but not for sports like golf!

Another turn of events that coincided conveniently with everything happening in my life was the invention of portable and wireless EEG Devices. An EEG (electroencephalogram) measures electrical activity in the brain, a practice that has been possible for approximately 100 years. It is typically measured in Hertz (Hz) or microvolts (UV) which is the amplitude of the Hz. The magic was not in the measurement itself but in the **wireless** measurement. I was now able to stand 6-12 feet away from any human trying to perform any task, cognitive or neuromuscular, or both, and look in real time into their brains. I had no idea that, as of this writing, I would have done over 18K of these and counting.

A sample of the non-clinical scans I have conducted includes investigations of brains performing tasks such as:

1. Shooting a free throw in basketball
2. Hitting all kinds of golf shots
3. Baseball player throwing a pitch
4. Baseball batter on deck and at bat
5. Quarterback throwing a football
6. Non-target sports athletes like Nascar, Swimmers, Runners, Cyclists, etc.
7. An executive thinking through a business decision
8. An artist trying to be creative
9. A youth diagnosed with ADD trying to focus on a school quiz or sport
10. ... and my Mom trying to recall a memory!

Looking exclusively at electricity initially (later technologies incorporated heart rate and brain oxygen levels), I began to see predictable patterns which are discussed in detail in Chapters 2 and 3. First, in Chapter 2, I explain the often-misunderstood path to achieving your goal. Every golfer wants to shoot lower scores—but what if the real key lay in rethinking how we approach the game itself? Essentially, every higher human ability (cognitive and neuromuscular) seems to occur in lower frequencies (10-20 Hz). This was not ground-breaking as it was already established in the neuroscience world, but I was seeing it myself firsthand. I elaborate on this in Chapter 3. This baseline data set in motion the most important question: **is it possible to get to this high performing state on command, anywhere, anytime, and especially in-the-game moments where traditional approaches are just not practical?** If a basketball player is on the free throw line with one second to go and the game on the line, he cannot call a timeout and go meditate for 30 minutes, return in that calm state, and take the shot. A golfer does not have time when over a seemingly makeable putt his brain is yelling at himself internally. What options are available in these all-too-common high-performance scenarios? Is it not in these moments, as the cliché goes, that champions are made? The sports world is full of cliches describing these situations: choking, managing nerves, under-the-gun, crunch time, digging deep, moment-of-truth. These bronze-age terms describe elevated levels of electricity both in the brain and traveling from the brain to neuromuscular functions. **In moments when time-outs are not available, new skills are required that only take seconds.** These are neurohacks and discussed in Chapter 4.

The answer to the critical question (**is it possible to get to this high performing state on command, anywhere, anytime, and especially in-the-game moments?**) is yes. The methodology and tools to do so are discussed in detail with examples and case studies in this book. This is that 'Upstream Fix' that was mentioned earlier.

It is worth noting that we may have been thinking about High Performance incorrectly to begin with. Regarding golf specifically, a good question to ask is, "How long do I need to be in this high performing state?" Is it really five hours (typical round of 18 holes of golf)? Are you hitting the ball all five hours? No! Between the time it takes for your pre-shot routine and hitting the ball, we are talking about less than 15 minutes out of five hours for when a golfer truly needs to be in this low frequency state. This is a very reasonable ask of self. To top it all, unlike almost any other sport, the game of golf gifts each golfer a "time-out" after each shot (time it takes to travel to next shot) where so much repurposing of time can be done that can make it even easier to get to low frequencies by the time you get to the next shot.

In this book, I give you simple language and tools to understand electricity in your brain. The language and tools are not just for golf. That same brain of yours that you use for golf is also used off the course in your life and you will be able to apply the tools in all parts of your life.

There were many accidental discoveries made when doing the 18K EEG scans. I have captured them in each relevant chapter.

One of them is my reasoning for why **Golf is the most difficult target sport** of all.

First, **Golf is a Target Sport:** the objective of the game of golf is to send the ball to a destination (target). This is very similar to other target sports. A football quarterback is throwing the ball to a receiver (target). A baseball pitcher is throwing the ball to a spot in the hitting zone. A soccer player is kicking the ball to a teammate (pass) or the goal. A basketball player similarly is passing the ball to a teammate or shooting at the basket. In these target sports, it is rare that these shots to targets do not have high quality visual input from the eyes. The eyes are either on the target or peripheral vision is high and, most importantly, the overall geospatial size of the performance arena is the same—it does not change. Games like soccer, basketball, football, and baseball are all played in the same field, respectively. Golf, on the other hand, is played over several hundred acres—essentially 18 unique 'fields'—so the role of the eyes is even more important to create a mental grid for targets. Even worse for golfers is that their eyes are never on the actual target out there, they are down on the golf ball in front of the club between their feet. This last visual imprint in the brain of the ball and its surrounding features (club head, shaft, feet, ball position, life of ball, color of ball, color of grass, etc.) are NOT the target, yet are dominating the Visual Cortex of the brain.

This makes the ability to recall the actual target while not looking at it the most important skill for golfers. I am aware this claim will rattle golfers and seasoned experts of the game. As such, I go deep into neuroscience to make this case in Chapter 5. I posit that without a target in the brain, the electricity shoots up as there is confusion on the instructions to the motor cortex from the visual cortex and this is the singular root cause of poor struck shots in golf, especially shots one is fully capable of executing.

In Chapter 6, I dedicate significant time to putting. Another surprise finding of all the measures I took was that there is a natural increase in electricity from Tee box to Green. I vividly recall the first time seeing this and thinking I was getting misreads on my device until I saw it happen repeatedly. It turns out, our subconscious is well aware that on every green on the golf course (18 of them), the following is a guarantee:

1. In a few seconds or imminently, a score will be determined, and it will be final and cumulative. This "spikes' the brain.
2. The margin of error is significantly smaller than any another golf shot. Off the Tee Box, one can miss the target by a yard or two and be fine, and the same on approach shots and possibly on greenside short game shots. But missing a putt by half inch is a full stroke! This awareness 'spikes' the brain.
3. It is the least neuromuscular motor sequence and application of force. The ball is sitting on the smoothest surface of the course, the putter has barely any loft and the sequence (backstroke to stroke) requires a precise (not violent/fast) movement to generate a force to send the ball to the target selected. This motor movement requires a matching electricity (low Hz) and for reasons #1 and #2, it is more difficult to get there.

It is my contention that, with a few exceptions, most putts inside 10 feet are very makeable. The PGA Tour Average from this distance is about 40%. I have no idea what this % is in non-tournament rounds, but I feel very comfortable saying it is not only higher, but significantly higher for these pros. It is my claim that the only reason this is as low as 40% is that there is too much mind share of the mechanics of the stroke and speed/line spiking electricity which in turn compromises that precise motor sequence required for that length putt.

In chapter 7, I explore the area where I am likely going to get the most push back: Practice time. I wrote about this in both my previous books. Given both the data I have since the last books as well as extensive new research on the role of the brain in memory formation, retention, and retrieval, it actually pains me to suggest that most of practice is useless – meaning, it is not useful. Parents/Coaches and range-ricks are not going to like this section as there is an implied truth that the more hours one spends practicing, the better one becomes. Of what value is, for example, two hours of practice putting if when you are playing, you cannot recall any value from that practice? 'Building Muscle Memory'—which is an argument often used for this—is an increasingly disputed claim from a purely neuroscience perspective.

Engaging in extended practice sessions offers other ancillary benefits, as this time is diverted from less productive activities such as playing video games or other activities that may negatively impact cognitive functions. But 'building muscle memory' by measuring the number of balls hit or hours spent is the least effective way. In Chapter 7, I go deep into using practice time to ENCODE the practice in such a manner that its retrieval is enhanced in the moments on the course when it is needed.

In Chapter 8, I argue that of all the things to do to be better at golf, especially for a tournament or competitive round (as opposed to a relaxed recreational round), none is more important than sleep and the nighttime routine that goes with it. I am a huge fan of Dr. Matthew Walker, Neuroscience professor at the University of California at Berkeley, whose work on sleep is groundbreaking. I did not get to do enough EEG scans in the mornings with subjects for obvious reasons, but there are enough wearable devices that track sleep to determine what a good or bad night of sleep is. I've used data from these third-party devices to then track shots (especially putting) and the results corroborate with Dr. Walker's research. It is the most important performance lever because there is just no substitute or adjustment to make for sleep, unlike other challenges where some kind of an adjustment in the middle of the round or tournament week can always be made.

Chapter 9 is a collaborative one. Golf coaches from around the world share how they have applied the concepts in these chapters into real life case studies. You will enjoy this chapter, and I am grateful to these amazing coaches who have enhanced their coaching repertoire with new tools. The last chapter is from Jim Hinckley, rated #5 Most Powerful Person in *Golf Inc. Magazine* (2022). His perspective as both a golfer and a major influencer at the highest levels of golf is a worthy read.

Because I am now aware that upstream is where the magic is—the brain—it was incumbent on me, not you, to write this book in such a manner that your brain can absorb the knowledge. Even though this is my ninth book, I wrote this book very differently from all my previous ones. Chapters are bite-size, points are in simple bullet points, examples and case studies are highlighted to enhance your attention, and the main chapters end with 'key takeaways' so that the points in the chapter can be stored more effectively, make it less likely to forget, and more likely to recall when you need it most!

I am in the back nine of my life now. My future is certainly shorter than my past. Please know I wrote this book with the intention to add to the body of knowledge regarding this amazing game of golf. I hope a few of you will take up neuroscience and continue to research the brain, for it is the most fascinating phenomenon in the universe. I hope research proves some of my claims correct, some incorrect but all well-intentioned to help us enjoy the game so it really is a challenge between you and the course, and not you and yourself.

02 | IT'S NOT A SECRET

Unlocking Your Best Mental State

It has never been easier to be physically healthy and at the same time, never been harder to be mentally healthy. Your mental health IS your performance.

The best place to start a book is by establishing what the goal is. What exactly is it that we want when playing golf? The obvious answer is to shoot lower scores and as the cliché goes, that is the result. What is the process to get to this goal? What is the secret? Is it a secret?

Questions: Have you played a round of golf at your best? What was your best score? When and where was it? Now make a list of six one-word attributes of what you were thinking or feeling or doing in your best round of golf (include location and date):

1. _____
2. _____
3. _____
4. _____
5. _____
6. _____

Here is a compilation of some athletes and historical figures describing their best performance:

Title: "The Perfect Game"

Athlete: Jake Reynolds
Event: Boston Marathon – April 17, 2023 – Boston, MA

*The roar of the crowd echoed as I surged up Heartbreak Hill. My legs burned, my lungs screamed, but my mind? It was calm. **Mental resilience** fueled me. I focused on my breath, repeating, "One more step." At mile 25, doubt whispered, but I silenced it with confidence built from months of training. With **unwavering focus**, I sprinted the last stretch, crossing the finish in a personal best—2:08:37. That day, it wasn't just strength; it was **belief, grit, and presence** that carried me to victory. My mind won the race before my body did.*

Title: "Mamba Mentality in Action"

Athlete: Kobe Bryant
Event: January 22, 2006 – Staples Center, Los Angeles, CA

*From the first shot, I knew. My focus was razor-sharp, my rhythm unstoppable. I wasn't thinking—I was **flowing**. Shot after shot, I drowned out the noise, locked into **relentless determination**. My teammates fed me the ball, and I delivered—**pure confidence, zero hesitation**. By the fourth quarter, I glanced at the scoreboard—81 points. But it wasn't about numbers. It was about **mind over fatigue, will over doubt**. That night, I proved what's possible when preparation meets **unshakable belief**. The game wasn't just won—it was mastered, one possession at a time. **Mamba Mentality**.*

Title: "The Comeback of a Lifetime"

Athlete: Tom Brady
Event: Super Bowl LI – February 5, 2017 – NRG Stadium, Houston, TX

*Down **28-3** in the third quarter, the world doubted us. But doubt never entered my mind. I told the guys, "One play at a time." **Mental toughness, composure, and belief**—that's what mattered now. We chipped away at the deficit, drive by drive, staying **locked in, emotionless, focused**. Overtime came. I stepped into the huddle, eyes sharp. **Confidence radiated**. A perfect drive. A perfect finish. **Victory**. Super Bowl champions. That night wasn't about talent alone—it was about **resilience, preparation, and unwavering faith** in the process. The greatest comeback in Super Bowl history was won in the mind first.*

Title: "Called Shot to Greatness"

Athlete: Babe Ruth
Event: Game 3, 1932 World Series – October 1, 1932 – Wrigley Field, Chicago, IL

*The crowd jeered, the Cubs' dugout taunted, but I just smirked. Stepping to the plate, I felt it—**unshakable confidence**. Two strikes. Then, I did it. I pointed to center field. **Was it a challenge? A prediction?** Maybe both. The next pitch came, and I swung with everything in me. **Crack**. The ball soared, clearing the center-field wall. A home run. The "Called Shot" was born. But that moment? It wasn't just skill. It was **belief, fearlessness, and showmanship**. When the pressure was highest, I didn't just play—**I owned the moment**. That's what legends do.*

Title: "The Rumble in the Jungle"

Athlete: Muhammad Ali
Event: October 30, 1974 – The Rumble in the Jungle – Kinshasa, Zaire

*They said Foreman was too strong. They said I was past my prime. But I knew something they didn't—**fighting isn't just muscle, it's the mind**. From the first round, I leaned back, let him swing, absorbing the punishment. **Rope-a-dope**. I whispered, "**Is that all you got, George?**" Round after round, he tired. My body* *ached, but my spirit?* **Unbreakable.** *Then, in the eighth—bam, bam, bam! A flurry. He staggered. One final right hand. Down he went. Victory. That night wasn't just about boxing—it was about* **strategy, patience, and an unshakable belief in myself.** *I was, and remain,* **The Greatest.**

Title: "The Conviction"

Athlete: Eric Liddell
Event: 400m Final – Paris Olympics – July 11, 1924

They doubted me. I wasn't supposed to win the 400 meters—I trained for the 100. But when I refused to run on Sunday for my faith, I was given a new race. **Adversity didn't weaken me—it fueled me.** *At the starting line, I whispered a verse:* **"He who honors me, I will honor."** *The gun fired. I ran—arms flailing, head back—* **pure will, unshakable faith.** *The others faded. My lungs burned, my legs screamed, but I never slowed.* **World record. Gold medal.** *That race wasn't just about speed—it was about* **conviction, belief, and heart.**

Title: "Champions Never Fade"

Athlete: Jack Nicklaus
Event: The Masters – April 13, 1986 – Augusta National, GA

They said I was too old, past my prime at **46 years old.** *But I knew better.* **Experience, patience, and belief—***that's what mattered now. I started the back nine, five shots back. Then, the putts started falling.* **Birdie. Birdie. Eagle.** *The roars echoed through Augusta. I stood over my* **18-foot putt on 17,** *heart steady.* **Clutch.** *A final birdie. A charge for the ages. When I walked off the 18th green,* **the sixth Green Jacket was mine.** *That Sunday wasn't just about skill—it was about* **focus, resilience, and proving that champions never fade.**

Title: "The Night the Stars Shone"

Artist: Vincent van Gogh
Event: June 1889 – Painting The Starry Night – Saint-Rémy-de-Provence, France

*The world saw me as lost, trapped in an asylum, but my mind was free. **Pain didn't break me—it fueled my art.** One night, I stood by my window, gazing at the swirling sky, the moon glowing like a beacon. **I felt something deep, something unspoken.** With every brushstroke, I poured out my soul—motion, emotion, light, life. The sky danced. The stars burned. By dawn, The Starry Night was born. It wasn't just paint on canvas—it was **passion, struggle, and vision.** They wouldn't understand in my lifetime, but I knew—I had captured something eternal.*

Title: "Greatness"

Great Person: Alexander the Great
Event: The Battle of Gaugamela – October 1, 331 BCE – Mesopotamia

*The dust rose, the air thick with the scent of war. Darius III's army outnumbered us, but numbers meant nothing. **Strategy, courage, and the will to win—those were my weapons.** I saw the gap in their lines. **This was the moment.** With a shout, I led my cavalry straight through, splitting the Persian forces. **Chaos. Fear. Collapse.** Darius fled, and the mighty Persian Empire was mine. But conquest was never just about war—it was about **vision, unity, and the pursuit of greatness.** That day, I didn't just win a battle—I changed the world forever.*

Title: "Let There be Light"

Inventor: Thomas Edison
Event: The Invention of the Practical Light Bulb – October 21, 1879 – Menlo Park, New Jersey

*The room was silent, filled with anticipation. **Thousands of failures led to this moment**. I adjusted the carbon filament, my hands steady. **This time, it would work.** The switch was flipped—a soft, **steady glow filled the lab.** We held our breath. **One minute. Five minutes. An hour.** It didn't burn out. **Victory.** The world would never be the same. People called me a genius, but the truth? **It was persistence, patience, and belief in possibility** that created this light. That night, darkness lost. And humanity stepped into a new era—**an era of innovation.***

Throughout time and history of competition, amazing performances have been delivered. In almost every case, they seem to have described the same attributes. Do you see them?

I have asked this question of countless athletes, coaches, artists, successful people, and amateurs alike: *What are you thinking, feeling, or doing when you are at your best?* They all give generally the same responses. Here is a summary of their Top Six one-word attributes:

1. Focused
2. Calm
3. Slow
4. Effortless
5. Not-thinking
6. Free

In this chapter, I need to convince you that the **attributes of your best version are not a secret**, and in fact, they have never been a secret in any human endeavor, not just in golf. Whatever you listed as your attributes earlier, finding ways to get there FIRST is key. By all means work on your swing, fitness, equipment, and course management, but to make what will make you perform your best on the golf course a secret is a self-inflicted falsehood. Whatever adjustment you have to make on the course, it must START with how far you are from these attributes and doing what you can to get back there.

No one calls me or people like me when they are playing or performing great. They call either when they are playing poorly or, often times, when they have hit rock bottom. So, I tend to meet athletes at their worst. I can tell you hands down, to a person, they all have one thing in common - no matter the sport: "**I have so many thoughts in my head!**" I look into their brains, and they are right—they are miles from being focused, calm, slow, effortless, and free. My singular goal is to get them back to this state, and then somehow, their athleticism resurfaces. They begin to react to the challenges of the shot as opposed to a flood of disabling memories.

A very fair question to ask at this point is that if the attributes of our best version are not a secret, and they never were to begin with, as attested by the short stories above, then why can we not get there on our own or on command? From a neuroscience perspective, I can tell you that having a very high level of awareness of the root causes of why you are not exhibiting high performing attributes is the key to learning to how to get to that state when you do need to.

Root Causes: Why Is It Hard to Get to A Focused State?

1. **The average EEG (noise in the brain) of a normal person today is the equivalent of that of a Schizophrenic from the 1940s/50s (Amen, 2015).**

    Since 2010, there has been an exponential explosion worldwide of mobile devices which are a source of constant cognitive stimulation. These devices have enabled a great deal of positive human experiences from the ability to communicate with anyone, anywhere, anytime, to finding support for anything, from accessing information to addressing any problem, to our banking and social interactions. To not have a device is a severely compromising lifestyle today. So, it is not an option to not have one, but this volume of stimulation is not what the brain was designed to consume.

    If a restaurant offered you all-you-can eat all day long for a low price and you get there early in the morning to eat all day, you would throw up by the time you got to dinner. Our digestive system was not designed to consume constant nutritional calories. In the same way, our brains were not designed to consume the volume of stimuli coming from mobile devices which are in our pockets wherever we go, easily accessible with a broad menu of options for digital information to consume. This is over stimulation.

2. **This over stimulation now means mega competition in your brain between all the stimulation already there (much of which is not processed in any healthy way) and low frequency sensory input.**

Think of a very stressful event you just finished on a normal day and now you're driving home. The radio is on, and it takes approximately 30 minutes to reach home. Because your brain is still processing the negativity from the event, it is highly unlikely that you will be able to hear the music playing or recall what you saw or heard on your drive home. Your sensory input, though very much open, cannot compete with the high frequency stimulation of the negative event in your brain. For golfers, imagine missing a 2-foot putt on the last hole and then driving home with music playing in the car. Would your brain be processing the missed putt or listening to the music?

In golf, this is why it is so difficult to recover from a poor shot. In watching dozens of junior golf events with my son, I witnessed juniors playing very well until a poor shot or score. It was predictable, based on their non-verbal behavior, that they were spiking. I could 'see' high frequency brain waves and knew their ability to get quality sensory input for the next shot was compromised. Anything from grip pressure, to feeling the wind or noticing the lie, to picking the wrong target or not even having a target, and such like results. Over-stimulated brains are prone to over-reacting to poor shots and not recovering well or making the right adjustments.

3. **Mind Wandering is 65%.** A Harvard Study by Matt Killingsworth found that Mind Wandering on average was at 65%. This means that because of over-stimulated brains, for 65% of your round of golf, your brain is elsewhere. If that 65% mind wandering occurs in your pre-shot routine or worse, over a shot, then the quality of your shot will be compromised. **Focus Time is down**

to about three seconds. That means the mind wandering is at 65% because every three seconds, the mind is being distracted … by itself.

Imagine if you were about to make a putt. About two seconds before you are about to start your stroke, someone nearby yells. Your brain has no choice but to consume that auditory input which means that your attention to the target or your intention of shot is replaced with this distracting thought. This increases the electricity in your brain because it wants to tell your motor cortex what to do but it is still processing the external auditory input. So, you're likely to hit a poor putt. I think most of us can relate to this logic. Now if this makes sense, then realize that **your brain is doing this to itself every three seconds.**

The distracting auditory input these days is not external, but internal and the result is the same confusion in communication from the brain to the neuromuscular functions. Consider the possibility that the self-distraction occurs not before your stroke but during your stroke. Imagine as you take your putter back, your brain says something like, "make sure you hit it hard because you left the last one short." This thought carries a very high level of electricity, and some form of neuromuscular disruption is certain to occur. I have seen and measured this in golfers who struggle with yips or are not able to have a smooth or rhythmic stroke. No new putter, putter grip, or stroke can fix distracting thoughts long term. There might be some placebo effects with trying something new, but the ability to manage these internal distractions is key and is discussed at length for putting in Chapter 4.

4. **Instant-shared Micro Trauma.** The ability to instantly and constantly share information via texting, social media, or other instant-messaging platforms (all in our hip pockets via a device) **has created a large inventory of negative stimuli (micro trauma) to consume.**

I grew up in Africa. I recall getting the *Time Magazine* that was a week old and looking at still pictures of perhaps an earthquake in another part of the world from possibly two weeks prior. The delay in the relay of this trauma, even though not of my own, diluted the impact (spike) on me. An earthquake today anywhere in the world, and I am likely to see hundreds of videos on multiple platforms. Still not my own trauma, but it is stimuli that my brain has to consume. Texting bad news in seconds of it happening to friends/family, perhaps even in group chats where multiple responses ensue, is infinitely more stimuli for brains to consume than previous times.

A 2020 study published in *Nature Communications* found that individuals who frequently encounter negative news on social media are more likely to experience symptoms of anxiety and depression. Additionally, a 2017 survey by the American Psychological Association reported that 56% of adults feel stressed by staying connected to social media and constant news updates. These findings suggest that the rapid dissemination of traumatic content via instant communication platforms can contribute to cumulative stress and emotional strain over time.

It is troubling to assert that it has never been easier to be more physically and technically sound in golf, and yet it has also never been harder to get to your high performing attributes, even though they are not a secret but because they are all cognitive. This is at the root of inconsistencies in performance. What changes from hitting good shots on the range to playing poorly on the first holes? What changes when you play a few holes well and not so on others? Your age, height, knowledge, skills, and desire will not change over a few hours. The change is in the electricity in your brain which is processing both current stimuli (situation), past stimuli (how you have been playing), and future stimuli (how you want to play in the remaining holes)—all of which is a big bully to your sensory cortex, compromising what you can see, feel, and giving your brain high quality information necessary for the shot at hand.

Golfers, coaches, instructors, parents, and caddies all need to understand that new skills are required for these new human challenges. These challenges are not a character flaw, but a cost of the human experience we have all found ourselves in. Part of the new skills are a deeper understanding of the brain, a new language to use on and off the course, and new skills to quickly 'spike down' those pesky distracting thoughts. This is the upstream fix that can make it easier to execute shots on the course that you are fully capable of executing.

If brand new golf clubs came to the market with a 100% guarantee that perfect shots will be executed with these clubs, hypothetically of course, I am certain everyone would buy them. If the manufacturer of the clubs said there was only one caveat: The guarantee is only valid if the clubs were in a good mood. I think most of us would laugh and despite the promise, would never put faith on equipment whose performance is based on their mood. Yet, this is exactly the standard that we have accepted with our brains. It is no secret that our lived experiences are better when we are in a good mood, and we play better. We have, however, normalized the idea that we are just going to play poorly when not in a good mood. It does not have to be this way.

In the next chapter, I go deep on the Neuroscience.

🔑 Key Takeaways

- The best version of you isn't a mystery — it's repeatable and recognizable.
- Peak performance is consistently described using the same mental attributes: calm, focused, effortless.
- Modern distractions make accessing those attributes more difficult than ever before.
- Overstimulation and internal mind-wandering are now the biggest barriers to good performance.
- Poor shots are often caused by internal distractions, not technique or physical skill.
- New tools are required to regulate brain activity and return to high-performing mental states.
- Mental performance is not a bonus skill — it's the foundation for consistency in golf.

Most of the shots you hit are not the reflection of your skill –
but of the noise in your head at the time of shot, most of which
is your repository of most recent similar poor shots.

03 | NEUROSCIENCE
– WHAT IS 10 HZ?

Brainwaves That Drive Performance

Many of the gains in golf techniques enabled by advances in technology are being eroded by over-stimulated distracted brains.

Santiago Ramón y Cajal and Fridtjof Nansen made pioneering contributions to neuroscience, fundamentally shaping our understanding of the nervous system. Cajal, using Golgi's staining technique, demonstrated that neurons are individual, separate cells — not a continuous network — forming the basis of the **neuron doctrine** (Kandel et al., 2013). Their combined insights shifted neuroscience away from reticular theory and toward modern cell-based models. For his work, Cajal shared the **1906 Nobel Prize in Physiology or Medicine** with Camillo Golgi. I have leveraged this understanding in studying neuroscience exclusively for sensory input and motor function. Understanding how electricity (polarity) is created in an individual neuron (given that there are 90 billion of them in the brain) has shaped my research and claims.

The term neuroscience is itself quite complex. Ten expert neuroscientists could be on stage, but all could likely be working on completely different parts or functions of the brain. Unlike other organs of the body, the brain has an enormous amount of responsibility coordinating multiple functions. The heart, kidney, liver, pancreas, stomach, lungs, and most organs essentially do one job respectively. The brain has to communicate with all these organs and coordinate the following:

- **Movement** – Controls voluntary and involuntary actions
- **Breathing** – Regulates oxygen intake automatically
- **Heart Rate** – Adjusts blood circulation needs
- **Memory** – Stores and recalls information
- **Emotions** – Manages feelings and reactions
- **Decision-Making** – Evaluates choices and consequences
- **Speech** – Processes language and communication
- **Balance** – Maintains posture and coordination
- **Sleep Cycles** – Controls rest and recovery
- **Problem-Solving** – Analyzes and finds solutions

For the purposes of this book, I am going to focus on the language of the brain: Electricity.

Why Electricity?

In the 1950s, Alan Hodgkin and Andrew Huxley conducted groundbreaking experiments on the giant axon of a squid uncovering how nerve impulses are generated and transmitted. By applying electrical stimulation, they recorded ionic currents across the axon membrane, discovering that the movement of sodium and potassium ions produced action potentials. Their work led to the creation of the Hodgkin-Huxley model, a mathematical description of the electrical characteristics of excitable cells. This model laid the foundation for modern neuroscience. For their profound insights into nerve function, Hodgkin and Huxley were awarded the Nobel Prize in Physiology or Medicine in 1963.

We know for sure that electricity generated in the brain enables motor function.

All motor function, like simply walking or moving your head left or right to view something, requires an underappreciated level of cognitive function and speed to generate the appropriate reaction. If there is a loud noise to your right, that auditory input has to be made sense of as some kind of an 'alarm' or possible threat very quickly. There is a big difference between loud noise sounds like children laughing and children crying. A geospatial assessment is done, and your head moves in exactly the right direction of where that sound came from to provide visual input to the brain for further analysis of the auditory input. All this is happening in microseconds and would qualify as 'miraculous' by most measures, yet this collaboration between sensory input, cognitive function and motor output is done all day long without any conscious thought. So, SPEED is the primary reason for why electricity is the language of the brain and neuromuscular output.

Now, if the motor output is a more nuanced desired output, like a motor sequence (golf swing, putting stroke), then reactionary output is minimized, and a more cognitive functionality is required. If the purpose of that neuromuscular sequence requires a precise amount of force to send the ball to a precise target, well then, the collaboration between the brain and motor function must be at a very high level. The language of this collaboration is electricity.

For the purposes of this book, I have grouped electricity into bands below:

- Theta: 4-8 Hz
- Alpha: 8-12 Hz
- Beta: 15-30 Hz
- Gamma: 30+ Hz

The above electric bands are measurable in real time as communication is occurring from a stimulus all the way through completion of a golf shot and even post shot as the brain evaluates the result. It is measured in Hertz (Hz), and I have measured the electricity in real time of golfers hitting all kinds of shots. I have found that my data corroborates with the data of dozens of previous researches on what kind of electricity facilitates that high level of collaboration between the brain and motor function.

Supporting Research

Research indicates that specific brain wave patterns, particularly alpha (8–12 Hz) and theta (4–8 Hz) rhythms, play a significant role in soccer performance, especially during tasks like penalty kicks. A study involving under-17 soccer players examined the relationship between brain activity and kicking performance (Palucci et al., 2022). Using a portable 64-channel EEG system, researchers measured brain oscillations in delta, theta, alpha, beta, and gamma frequency bands across various brain regions during different phases of the kick. The findings revealed that both ball velocity and placement accuracy were moderately associated with individual EEG oscillations. Specifically, occipital alpha oscillations were found to have significant predictive power regarding the magnitude of error in placing the ball in the goal.

Research has also demonstrated a significant correlation between specific brain wave patterns — particularly alpha (8–12 Hz) and theta (4–7 Hz) rhythms — and successful golf putting performance. A study published in *Frontiers in Psychology* investigated the neural activity of golfers during putting tasks, focusing on these frequency bands (Zhang et al., 2022). The findings revealed that superior putting performance was linked to distinct patterns in theta and alpha power, suggesting that these brain wave activities play a crucial role in the preparation and execution of successful putts.

Another 2022 study published in *Frontiers in Neuroergonomics* investigated the effects of high-definition transcranial direct current stimulation (HD-tDCS) on basketball free-throw shooting performance. The research involved professional female basketball players and aimed to understand how modulating brain activity could influence sports performance. The findings indicated that HD-tDCS could affect neural mechanisms relevant to sports performance, particularly during tasks like free-throw shooting.

These results suggest that interventions targeting specific brain regions can influence performance in sports requiring precision and focus, such as basketball and golf.

Even in other areas of human performance, it appears that the electrical bands of alpha and theta play a key part in producing higher abilities.

Research shows that increasing **alpha (8–12 Hz) and theta (4–8 Hz) brain wave activity** enhances cognitive functions like **creativity, innovation, problem-solving, imagination, and mental flexibility** (Gruzelier, 2014). These states are linked to **relaxation, visualization, and insight**, key factors for artists and innovators.

Creativity flourishes when the mind is **calm yet alert**, allowing ideas to flow effortlessly. Artists, writers, and entrepreneurs benefit from **alpha-theta training**, as it promotes **original thinking and breakthrough ideas**. Harnessing these states can **enhance cognitive performance**, making them valuable tools for innovation and creative success.

It turns out that what was discussed in Chapter 2 is very measurable. These were the Top Six attributes stated in my research of when athletes performed at their best:

1. Focused
2. Calm
3. Slow
4. Effortless
5. Not-thinking
6. Free

The attributes you listed as well as the above anecdotally referenced in all high performing human endeavors going back centuries are all related to specific electrical frequency: Alpha and Theta Brain Waves. This seems to be the best brain 'language' for all activities, but especially for those requiring motor output where accuracy is desired, which is essentially all target sports. I will take some liberty and average alpha and theta bands to 10 Hz (which coincidentally is the name of my other book and podcast: *Chasing 10 Hz*).

Let's redo the above attributes now in terms of the electrical frequency:

Figure 1.

Mental State at 10Hz

Focused = 10 Hz   ⟶   ⟵   Calm = 10Hz

Slow = 10Hz   ⟶   ⟵   Effortless = 10Hz

Not-thinking = 10Hz   ⟶   ⟵   Free = 10Hz

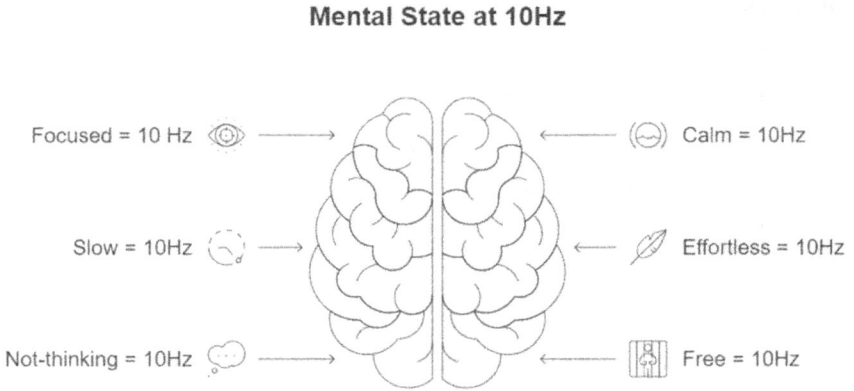

So, **chasing 10 Hz is really the goal**, especially for precision tasks (like putting) as well as high order of decision-making and focus. As discussed in Chapter 2, my claim is that it has never been harder to get the brain to 10 Hz because the sheer volume of stimulation constantly being fed to the brain and the intensity of that stimulation puts the brain baseline (starting point) at significantly higher elevated electrical states. This is in large part the root cause of poor sleep, which is discussed in Chapter 8.

Are there ways you can know, even if in general terms, what is the electrical state of your brain? Yes! Thoughts, feelings, and behavior provide valuable clues to making very good guesses without the need for an EEG device on your head.

Here's a table of those clues:

Table 1.

FREQUENCY (HZ)	THOUGHTS	FEELINGS	BEHAVIOR
30+ HZ	1. "Not my day!" 2. "I can't stand this!" 3. "What!!" 4. "I Suck!!" 5. "I'm Done with this!"	1. Angry 2. Confused 3. Helpless	1. Complaining. 2. Blaming others. 3. Looking Down. 4. Yelling. 5. Cussing. 6. Walking/taking fast.
15-30 Hz	1. Not sure but I think this is right. 2. Thinking about other parts of life (distracted) 3. Can't seem to hit shots i normally hit. 4. Recalling past poor shots.	1. Indifferent. 2. Blend of both highs and lows. 3. Not really caring.	1. Very Inconsistent blend of above and below.
10 Hz	1. I have a good target. 2. I know what to do. 3. I'm fully committed. 4. I can sense my grip, see dimples on ball	1. Happy. 2. Peaceful. 3. Relaxed. 4. Calm 5. Free	1. Slow. 2. Not Rush. 3. Good rhythm/tempo. 4. Not overreact. 5. Good Decisions. 6. Calm verbal monologue and dialogue.

Self-awareness of your thoughts, feelings, and behavior is a necessary skill for high performance. Knowing what you're thinking, feeling, and how you are behaving is powerful knowledge as it directs you to get back to 10 Hz with the right adjustments. If you're at 60Hz for example, you would want to do something very powerful and quick to get to 10 Hz. If you're at 20 Hz, a lesser intervention might be more appropriate. If you're at 10 Hz, like a baseball pitcher pitching a no hitter, nothing is required and the reason they are left alone in the dugout between innings!

Electricy can also be measured using an MRI machine (as opposed to an EEG device). The brain scans in each of the bands above are quite vivid, even in non-functional states (not doing a task) but still monitoring brain activity as it processes high stress, normal, and high performing thoughts. In these scans, in the images of the brain, colors are often used to label these states, much like colors are used on a weather app for radar maps. In weather radar maps, Red, Yellow, Green and clear depict states of intensity with red being high intensity and yellow/green indicate lesser intensities of the weather. In a brain MRI scan/image, the identical labels are used, as noted in the next figure.

Figure 2.

Color Coding MRI Brain Scan Frequencies

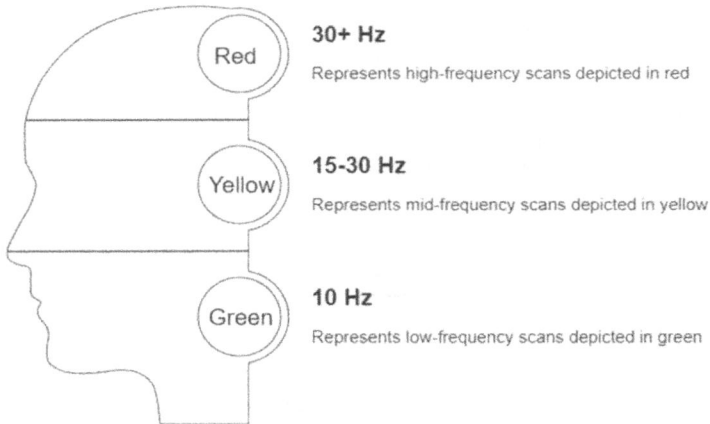

30+ Hz

Represents high-frequency scans depicted in red

15-30 Hz

Represents mid-frequency scans depicted in yellow

10 Hz

Represents low-frequency scans depicted in green

It is coincidental that these colors match a traffic light. As I work with coaches/athletes, I have found these color labels to be far more effective in self-awareness. They are less judgmental than the Emotional, Cognitive, or even Behavioral labels in the previous table. The brain responds more favorably when the label of its state is Red, Yellow, or Green versus Angry, Indifferent, or Happy. Colors are agnostic and the real purpose should be to quickly label the thought and feeling and make an adjustment to get back to Green (10 Hz). Moving forward, I will use the terms Red, Yellow, and Green to capture the general state of the brain. You are strongly encouraged to use these colors in your Self-Awareness. Having only three labels to choose from when playing will make it easier to assess where you are, eliminate the counter-productive and spiking thoughts of trying to figure out what emotional label to use, and recruit less judgmental thoughts.

Note: The Brain is not actually Red, Yellow, or Green. It is a white/brown blend.

So, what exactly is magical at 10 Hz? Why is this low-level amplitude of electricity so good for the communication between cognitive functions of the brain and motor output?

There are two amazing outcomes in Green, at 10 Hz: (1) Amplification of Sensory Input, and (2) Enhanced Quality of Decision-Making.

1. Amplification of SENSORY INPUT

In lay terms, when there is less noise in our heads, we think clearer. Noise is a lot of thoughts (quantity) and high intensity of thoughts. Golfers claim that one of the more common attributes of their best rounds (high performance) is that they were "not thinking." This is not factually accurate or even possible since the brain is always thinking. What they are really saying is that they are not thinking in Yellow or Red—the high intensity thoughts. Being in Green (10 Hz) feels like no thoughts because **Sensory Input** is dominating in the brain due to little 'traffic' or competing higher frequency electricity.

Sensory input—what you're seeing with your eyes or feeling with your hands/feet/body—inherently carries lower frequency than a cognitive thought. A cognitive thought could be as simple as 'keep your head still' – this thought is coming from your memory bank (hippocampus) and is being retrieved along with so many other attached memories, likely a reminder because of some previous mishaps. Memories are inventories and the supply chain process of recruiting memories (cognitive thoughts) usually comes with other memories attached to it, usually not positive ones. This is why technical thoughts during a swing/stroke **feel** 'distracting' or 'heavy' – because they are a higher frequency and, as a result, they overpower sensory input.

Compare this cognitive input to sensory input during swing/stroke. If you FEEL the putter head and SEE exactly the spot where the ball is going to enter the hole, this sensory information is related to the exact present moment. Thus, the cliché "being in the moment" or "being present" is used when playing well. The FEELING of the putter head or the VISUAL blade of grass over which the ball needs to roll to go into the hole have little inventory attached to it. They don't have any history. What did the blade of grass ever do to you? Nothing!

It is for this reason that the QUALITY of sensory input leads directly to the QUALITY of motor output. The claim here is that High Quality Sensory Input = High Quality Motor Output.

Figure 3.

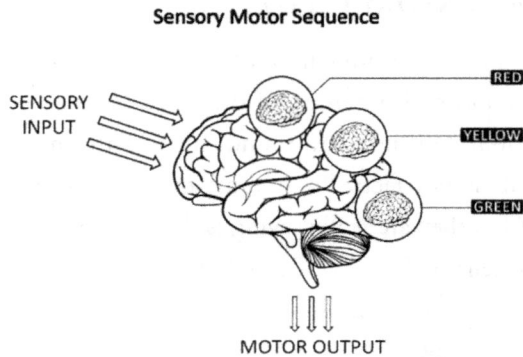

Sensory Motor Sequence

In Figure 3, you can see that high quality sensory input is given to the brain, which in turn communicates via electricity traveling on our nervous system (nerves). Electricity is 'carrying' the communication to the muscles to sequence motor pattern, to generate the right amount of force to send the ball to the target with high levels of precision. At 10 Hz, in Green, the way you have trained (your skills) to execute that shot will have a high degree of being replicated on the course in competition.

In a Princeton study, seminary students preparing to give a talk on "The Good Samaritan" passed a staged beggar *en route* (Darley & Batson, 1973). Despite their topic, many ignored him — especially when rushed. The study showed **situational pressure outweighed moral intent**, revealing how context, not just belief, drives behavior. In golf, situational pressure (context) will outweigh talent.

There is an inherent design of the human brain, however, that compromises this process. Sure, it would be nice if we lived in sensory mode all the time, but the factory setting of the brain is designed to assign meaning or context to the situation at hand, on and off the golf course. This context is not coming from the internet search engine nor objectively without any bias, it comes from our own search engine and hard drive—which regrettably is the inventory of our past experiences, good and bad.

Your brain knows the context of a practice putt on the putting green. It is largely meaningless because it will not be counted towards your score. Therefore, the inventory being retrieved is carrying much lower intensity electrical charge than if that same putt was on the first hole for par. Your brain knows the context of this putt for par and the following sample thoughts are retrieved from your internal search engine:

1. Don't want to start with bogey.
2. I was leaving a few short on the practice green to get this to the hole.
3. I always start poorly.
4. I can't believe I ran the first putt this far by.
5. I see a perfect spot right on the cup where this ball needs to enter the hole.

As a golfer, you can relate to all the above. Each one of the ascribed meanings (context) by the brain is carrying a different electric charge. All the examples above except for #5 are well above 10 Hz.

In the next chart (Figure 4), I was able to match thoughts to electrical frequencies and then correlate to the probability of making the putt (% Make). **The claim here is that the higher above 10 Hz the spike in electricity, the greater the probability of a neuromuscular disruption.**

Figure 4.

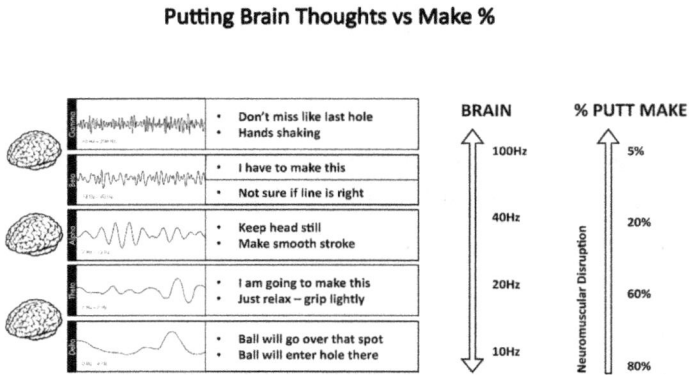

Putting Brain Thoughts vs Make %

Brain wave	Thoughts	BRAIN	% PUTT MAKE
	• Don't miss like last hole • Hands shaking	100Hz	5%
	• I have to make this • Not sure if line is right	40Hz	20%
	• Keep head still • Make smooth stroke		
	• I am going to make this • Just relax – grip lightly	20Hz	60%
	• Ball will go over that spot • Ball will enter hole there	10Hz	80%

(Neuromuscular Disruption)

A Neuromuscular Disruption is any physical motor pattern that was not intended. This disruption occurs on a motor sequence (skill) that you already have and have demonstrated before. For putting, it could be anything from hitting a putt harder or softer than you intended or hitting the ball off center of the putter face, or worse of all, shaking during your putting stroke. None of these disruptions were intentional, and no one wirelessly sent a surge of electricity to you.

Even though I only have data for putting above, I have measured similar thoughts in other parts of the game (Tee shots, Approach Shorts, Short game shots) as well as other sports and the results are strikingly similar.

Non-sensory input (context) is always attached to every shot in your round. It is for this seemingly obvious fact that I make claims in Chapter 7 (Practice) that most practice time is useless because, in part, there is no context attached to practice shots yet there is always high frequency context attached to in-round shots. This is the same reason why it is difficult to take range work or a good warm up into the round and why the first Tee shot on the first hole feels so different from other shots because it is the first context shot and the first electric spike. This clogs up sensory input creating a few uncomfortable feelings.

Later in this chapter I discuss specific techniques to 'spike down' those thoughts long enough to get towards 10 Hz or near it to execute the shot at hand, no matter the spike from distracting thoughts.

2. Enhanced Quality of Decision-Making

The second equally powerful magic of being in 10 Hz (Green) is the enhanced quality of cognitive functionality.

A competitive golfer must constantly engage in **high-level cognitive functions** to make strategic decisions throughout a round. Here are the top 10:

1. **Club Selection** – Choosing the right club for distance, conditions, and shot type
2. **Shot Shape Decision** – Deciding on a draw, fade, or straight shot based on obstacles
3. **Course Management** – Strategizing hole-by-hole to avoid hazards and maximize efficiency
4. **Reading Greens** – Analyzing slope, speed, and grain for optimal putting lines
5. **Risk vs. Reward Assessment** – Weighing aggressive vs. conservative shots based on position
6. **Wind & Weather Adjustments** – Factoring in wind speed, direction, and rain effects on ball flight
7. **Lie Assessment** – Evaluating ball position in rough, sand, or fairway for shot execution
8. **Emotional Regulation** – Managing pressure, frustration, and confidence to maintain performance
9. **Pre-Shot Routine Execution** – Visualizing the shot and committing to the process
10. **Time Management** – Pacing shots effectively to stay focused while maintaining tournament rules

Each decision requires quick and easy ACCESS to your hard drive of practice, skills, and past experience. This inventory exists only in your brain (hippocampus), and it quite miraculously is right next to both the Thalamus (where all sensory input goes) as well as the Amygdala (where emotions are created). When in Green, the traffic (noise) is low and you're likely to recall/notice everything about the shot required, inventory your best shots, and make a better decision on shot and target selection. Conversely, when in Red, the quality of sensory will be low, and coupled with elevated electrical frequency, you're likely accessing a very limited inventory of your skills and even your worst shots in similar circumstances. This 'fear' state will release neurotransmitters, like slow-acting Cortisol and much faster-acting Epinephrine, stress hormones, and further 'blind' the golfer from the target. Thinking and motor sequence are always faster. The default noticeable behavioral tendencies in this state are:

- Quick walking
- Negative verbalizations
- Faster swings especially in transition
- Hitting shots with faster swing speeds unintentionally
- Looking down

So, getting to Green (10 Hz) has a very powerful impact on both the quality of sensory input (which determines quality of motor output) and on decision-making by providing access to knowledge and skills you already have acquired (stored only in your brain).

🔑 Key Takeaways

- The brain operates through electrical signals, with 10 Hz linked to peak performance in sports and creativity.
- Alpha and Theta brain waves (8–12 Hz) are essential for calm, focused, high-performance states.
- At 10 Hz, sensory input is amplified, improving motor control and "feel" during performance.
- Higher brain frequencies (15–30+ Hz) correlate with stress, distraction, and reduced accuracy in target-based sports.
- 10 Hz also enhances decision-making by improving access to stored knowledge and reducing emotional interference.

- The brain assigns context to shots, increasing mental noise unless regulated consciously.
- Self-awareness of thoughts, feelings, and behaviors helps you identify your brain state and return to Green (10 Hz).

The amount of time it takes to hit a high-quality shot after a poor one is the measure of your mental game.

04 | NEUROHACKS

Quick Techniques to Quiet Noise

The brain will distract itself from any current task every 3-10 seconds. In a pre-shot routine that takes 60 seconds, that is 6-20 times. Just building self-awareness of what your brain is processing during this time will reduce the distraction.

The next question is, *how could a golfer spike down the electrical surges inherent in distracting thoughts?*

A good place to start to answer this question is to process how we spike down day-to-day stressors off the golf course. Are there techniques off the golf course that reduce stress (spike down)? Sure, there are. Some common techniques we all use are:

- Vacation
- Meditation practice
- Physical exercise
- Nature walk
- Healthy nutrition
- Power nap
- Gratitude journaling
- Social connection
- Listening to Music
- Cooking
- Watching Movie/Shows

- Reading
- Calling friends
- Visit friends
- Mindful stretching

We may have not thought of these techniques as neurohacks, but what they all have in common is low frequency activities (non-stress) and a time period of amplified sensory input.

These off-the-course spike-downs are great but not very practical when a distracting thought enters your brain in your pre-shot routine, or worse, when over the ball about to start your backswing/stroke. Are there other sensory techniques that take significantly less time (in seconds) and can be done with no equipment to have a similar spike down effect? This was a great question to explore.

The answer lay, ironically, in my Physics background. When electricity is traveling through a wire, we can measure the voltage.

The basic equation is Ohm's Law: Voltage = Current X Resistance (V = IR).

In my college lab work, I recollected having the ability to impact voltage by changing the resistance. In many cases, current could not be changed because it was a default Amperes (A) coming out of a source. So, R was an easier variable to adjust. We used the following tools to impact voltage in the hardwired electrical world:

1. Resistors

- o **Fixed Resistors** – Provide a constant resistance to drop voltage
- o **Variable Resistors (Potentiometers)** – Adjust resistance to control voltage output

2. Voltage Dividers

- o **Series Resistor Networks** – Two or more resistors in series to split voltage
- o **Adjustable Voltage Dividers** – Use variable resistors to fine-tune voltage drops

3. Rheostats

   o **High-power variable resistors** - Used in circuits to reduce voltage dynamically

4. Thermistors

   o **Temperature-sensitive resistors** - Lower voltage depending on heat conditions

5. Load Resistors

   o **Power resistors** - Used to safely dissipate excess electrical current, preventing circuit overload and simulating normal electrical load conditions

I began to explore what "R" could be in the brain to 'resist' the surge of electricity in the brain impacting neuromuscular sequence and application of force. I knew there was some kind of role that sensory input should have similar to the traditional off-the-course techniques.

I discovered that there is a system that manages the overall EEG (noise) in the brain that works a little independently, called the Vagus Nerve (VN). This system is the "military" system of the body where once a threat is recognized, real or perceived, all the "military" systems of the body are activated.

When the **Vagus nerve** detects a **threat**, it interacts with multiple organs and glands to regulate the body's **fight-or-flight** and **freeze responses**. Here are the Top 10 activated:

1. **Heart** – Regulates heart rate and blood pressure
2. **Lungs** – Controls breathing rate and depth
3. **Adrenal Glands** – Releases cortisol and adrenaline
4. **Gut (Intestines)** – Affects digestion and gut motility
5. **Stomach** – Slows digestion under stress
6. **Liver** – Manages glucose release for energy
7. **Spleen** – Modulates immune response

8. **Pancreas** – Regulates insulin and glucose levels
9. **Esophagus** – Influences swallowing and reflexes
10. **Kidneys** – Adjusts blood filtration and stress hormones

These are all the organs associated with stress and subsequent electrical spikes. All those off-course stress-relieving habits deactivate this Vagus Nerve system. They are the "R" in Ohm's Law.

What did those off-course stress-relieving habits have in common? Well, the answer was right in front of me. **They all provided the brain with low frequency high quality sensory input.** There is, in effect, a methodology where we CAN "demilitarize" these organs. Introducing the concept of neurohacks.

Neurohacks are proven self-inducing sensory stimuli that deactivate the Vagus Nerve, thereby diluting the threat perception and relieving the body of all its threat responses.

Neurohacks are always-available on-demand 'noise-cancellation' or 'performance-boosting' stimuli. Neurohacks tell the brain that the threat is not real, and the 'military' systems can stand down. A real threat is one where your life is in real danger, like a lion coming to eat you. Making a 6-foot putt to win a tournament or breaking your best score is certainly important, but it is not an existential threat that requires all your 'military' systems fully activated. It is important to you to make that putt. The context you have to that putt, however, has activated your brain's high alert system. This is a factory setting that, though necessary for real threats, needs to be deactivated quickly and long enough to get the electricity back towards Green (10 Hz) to execute the motor sequencing (putting stroke) that you already know how to do and send the ball to the target that you selected.

Neurohacks are a quick "R" in Ohm's Law that can spike down the surge of electricity that the context of a shot inherently generates.

Our five senses are always with us. We do not need to go anywhere to see something; we simply open our eyes and direct our gaze towards the object of interest. We do not have to go somewhere to feel what is under our feet or rub our thumbs on our fingers or our tongue inside our mouth. Also, using senses to deactivate the Vagus Nerve takes seconds. How long does it take to rub your fingers together? Or to look at the shape of a cloud? These are both self-induced sensory inputs to the brain that would never be done if the danger is real danger (existential threat). You would never look at a cloud and notice its shape if a lion was charging at you! By doing them over a putt, these self-inducing stimuli spike down the electrical surges that are guaranteed to occur in every round of golf because every shot will have a context that carries a higher frequency of electricity.

My team and I have developed dozens of neurohacks, all of which take seconds and are easy to self-induce, especially if you have developed a high degree of self-awareness using simple colors (Red, Yellow, Green).

Take a look at the next chart (Figure 5) from an actual person at a typical workplace during a typical workday. She tracked her Brain Temperature (Red, Yellow, Green) based on the tasks she had to perform throughout the course of the day. The smaller dots are Green emotions/thoughts, Yellow is shown in dashed line and Red in solid line. You see that giving feedback to an employee and at the end of the day were her two big spikes. You can also see that because she is in the flow of the workday, she does not have much time as she has subsequent events/tasks to perform. During this day, her options to spike down are very limited.

Figure 5.

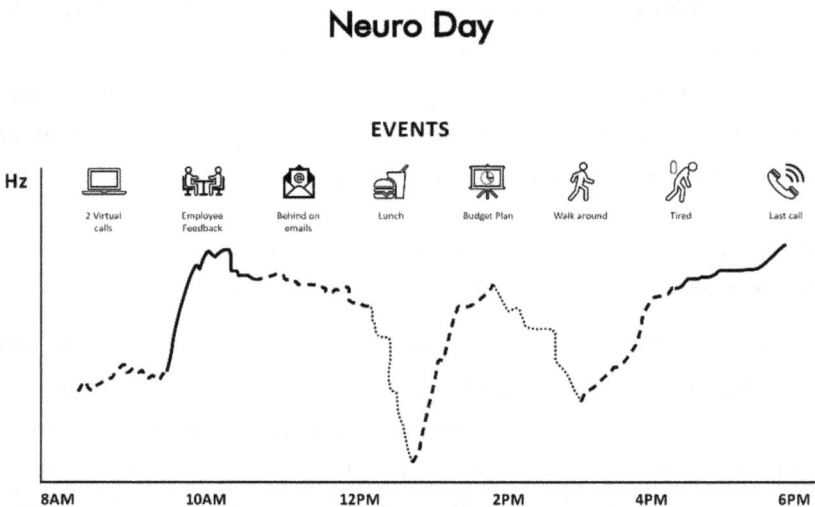

Neuro Day

EVENTS

| Hz | 2 Virtual calls | Employee Feedback | Behind on emails | Lunch | Budget Plan | Walk around | Tired | Last call |

8AM   10AM   12PM   2PM   4PM   6PM

A round of golf is no different. Good shots are inherently going to spike you down and poor shots are going to spike you up. In addition, your spikes may also be distracting thoughts in your pre-shot routine. In these spike moments, a new set of skills are needed to spike you down so as to minimize the impact of that spike on the next golf shot. Traditional techniques listed at the start of this chapter are great and recommended, but they are not pragmatic during your round of golf.

In 2024, I partnered with Dr. David Voran to conduct a study at the University of Missouri, Kansas City (UMKC). We tracked 10 medical doctors during the course of their shift (6-10 hours continuously) using a third-party wireless EEG device and my Neuro580 App over three consecutive days. This app provided customized neurohacks when a physician accessed it on their mobile phone and noted their color state (e.g., Red). An amazing treasure trove of data was captured: 32 data points per second, tracking multiple EEG frequencies from different parts of the brain, and Heart Rate resulting in over 11 Million data points of the brain at work through real-life ups and downs in a stress environment (hospital). As of this publication, more on this study and the Neuro580 App is available at www.neuro580.com.

The study also corroborated my previous 18K functional scans. The following image (Figure 6) is a reading from an actual golfer showing the state of the electricity three minutes before doing a neurohack and three minutes after.

Figure 6.

Golfer X Study

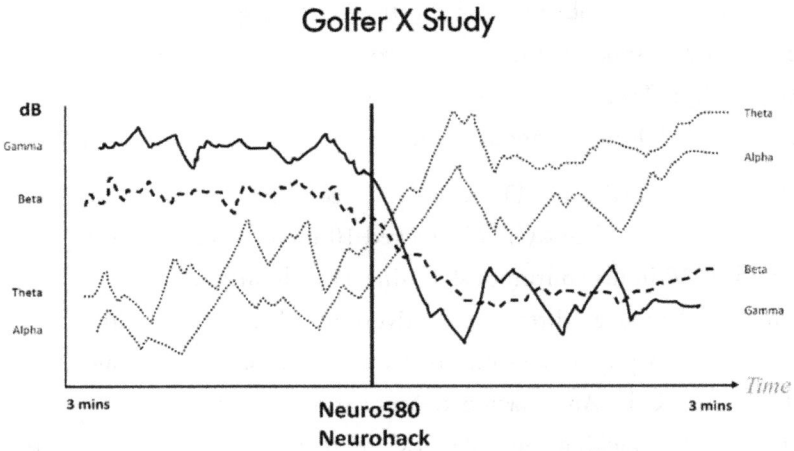

The high stress bands (Gamma/Beta, Red/Yellow) of EEG (stress) go down, and the high focus bands (Alpha/Theta, Green) go up. This is exactly the result of the hypothesis of inducing a "resistance" during a surge to spike down electricity.

A good question to ask is, *how long is the impact of the neurohack?* Well, it depends on many variables such as the level of the initial surge, sleep night before, number of surges prior, amount of time before the next surge, etc. But make no mistake, whether it is a few seconds to several minutes, this is enough time to execute the next task at hand. Given that these neurohacks take seconds and can be done anywhere using your senses, they should seriously be considered as part of every athlete's repertoire of skills for both in and out of competition spikes that competition—and life—will throw at you.

The Neuro580 App has a full library of these sensory neurohacks. Off the golf course, or in practice, two other forms of neurohacks are also provided: a low-frequency thought (like a mantra or inspiring quote) as well as a visual image that can trigger a spike down of EEG Brain Activity (like that of a favorite vacation or family member). But in competition, you will only need the self-inducing sensory input neurohacks.

An advanced skill is to learn which neurohack to use appropriately. When RED, a faster-acting (quick spike down) is needed than when Yellow. It is recommended to use different ones so as to not dilute the value of all of them. Save the Red neurohacks for 'emergency' situations on the course (like after missing a 2-foot putt or after hitting a ball OB). Missing a fairway by two yards or a 15-foot does not require a Red neurohack! Yellow ones can be used in these scenarios.

For the purposes of this book, only a few are shared here.

RED Neurohack: Slow Breath, Walk & Thoughts

Surges in context create surges in electricity making everything feel faster. The Resistance here (R) to reduce the voltage is **slowing** controllable neuromuscular motor sequences which send very powerful signals to the brain to deactivate the Vagus Nerve. You can do this by:

1. **Taking more breaths slowly in inhales and exhales.** This conscious controlled neuromuscular action will send signals to your brain that you are not in real danger.
2. **Walk Slow.** I understand that you have to keep walking (moving) in golf to your next shot but given the opportunity, just take steps at a slower pace. Even a slightly slower intentional pace feeling your feet (sensory input) than what you are subconsciously doing will increase R to reduce spiking Voltage.
3. **Think Slow.** I often have my golfer hum a song or tune very slowly as though the battery on their radio is dying and the music is coming out real slow. Because this is again a self-inducing stimulus to the brain, it reduces the spike surges.

Note: Once a tournament starts, everything feels faster. Context is being attached to all shots; the brain is naturally spiking. I have had countless conversations where golfers of all levels have told me that "things speed up" in competition and even though there is a walk involved between shots and it is five plus hours, it just feels fast. It is important to understand this phenomenon from a neurological perspective.

One second is always one second. It is just that—whether you are at the beach taking a nap or playing golf. Yet, golfers and athletes in general are right in observing that "it just feels faster." Recall one of the attributes of high performance in Chapter 2 is 'slow' where time feels slower.

The more brain waves and/or the more intense (higher frequency, Hz) brain waves, the faster time feels. This is because once a round begins, the sheer volume of new stimuli is dramatically more. There are just more stimuli (and real consequences) for your brain to process. The presence of more stimuli in conjunction with a game-time clock is suddenly much higher for the brain to process creating spikes. What is fast is too many stimuli to process, too many decisions to make, and being on the clock at the same time.

RED Neurohack: 10-2 Tension

If the context is enormous, the surge of electricity will be high. Along with everything feeling fast in Red is the loss in calibration of force. With too many stimuli to process (spikes), the brain has too much competition to be accurate with its sense of speed (how fast/slow to hit the ball) and force (how hard/easy to hit the ball).

Grab any club if it is near you and if not, take your hands and put them over each thigh. Now squeeze as hard as you can for about five seconds and 'record' what that tension felt like all over your body. Give that recording a 10. Then as SLOWLY as is humanly possible, release the grip pressure (tension) until it feels like a two (gentle soft tension).

It takes about 10 seconds to do this neurohack. This can be done in the middle of any pre-shot routine as long as your self-awareness is there regarding the threat rating of your distracting thought (spike).

I do not recommend you do a 10-2 if you are Green or even Yellow. Why not? If it works so well, then why not use it all the time? Well, because you want to save it for those guaranteed Red spikes like when over a key shot or after a missed short putt.

YELLOW Neurohack: 5-S

If feeling Yellow, this neurohack is recommended.

Activating the five senses in sequence: Smell-Taste-Sound-Feel-Sight. The idea is to find only one attribute from the present moment in the specific place you are for each sense. It should take no more than a few seconds and will spike down electricity, reducing the intensity of higher frequency (negative) brain waves.

This is a neurohack that can be used anywhere on the course during the round, at any time, but especially recommended for short-game shots.

YELLOW Neurohack: T&E – Talk with Eyes

Verbally (out loud to yourself or within your inner monologue) is the neurohack that I simply call "talking with eyes" using the 'T&E' acronym. An example of the T&E neurohack is:

I want to start the ball to be left of that bunker, past that mound, and let the wind move it right.

Consider all the visual sensory input this verbalization neurohack gives your brain! That is a lot of R to the electricity.

Note that talking with your eyes is not quite the same as visualization. The latter is not bad, but the verbalization of the visualization is much better.

Another EEG device manufacturer wanted to test these neurohacks independently in functional tasks (non-clinical) using their own device (www.neuro580.com). Their technology tracked three biomarkers:

1. EEG (Brain Electrical Activity)
2. Heart Rate
3. Oxygen in Brain (integrated Oximeter)

The triple-combo of these biomarkers is what they defined as the popular FLOW STATE from a percentage metric.

Note: *The term "flow state" was coined by Hungarian-American psychologist Mihaly Csikszentmihalyi in 1975. He introduced this concept after observing artists who became*

47

so absorbed in their work that they would lose track of time and basic needs. Csikszentmihalyi described flow as a mental state where individuals are fully immersed in an activity, experiencing energized focus and enjoyment.

The results are shown in the following Table 2.

Table 2.

3rd Party Study: BlueberryX (Canada)

Flow State: EEG + HR + OXYGEN

Neuro580 Neurohack	Activity Time (seconds)	FLOW STATE Pre Neurohack %	FLOW STATE Post Neurohack %	HEART RATE Pre Neurohack (bpm)	HEART RATE Post Neurohack (bpm)
10-2	10s	36	107	76	83
3F (neck roll)	10s	27	89	65	52
3F (Finger)	10s	29	81	76	61
3F (Toes)	10s	25	81	77	59
W2-60	60s	28	91	90	74
Tongue20	20s	18	66	83	68
Hum30	30s	27	91	68	86
3E (Picture)	10s	18	79	82	89
Wrist5	10s	34	63	80	72
4-2-8 Breath	10s	34	45	87	84

Traditional Neurohacks (Yoga, Meditation, Working Out, Listening to Music, Hobbies, etc) are great but require logistics and take too long to integrate in the-moment, anywhere, anytime.

The first column is just some of the neurohacks from a library of neurohacks I created and tested. The second column is the approximate amount of time it takes to perform the neurohack. You can see just how powerful these neurohacks are in giving immediate stress relief—useful for situations that golfers and athletes are guaranteed to find themselves in multiples times in a round.

Another powerful study in 2017 by Stavrakis et al. demonstrated that low-level vagus nerve stimulation (LLVNS) significantly reduced postoperative atrial fibrillation (POAF) in 58 cardiac surgery patients. In this randomized study, 26 patients performed LLVNS post-surgery and 22 did not. All 26 patients who performed these neurohacks (LLVNS) had lower levels of Blood Pressure and Inflammation. The study also found that LLVNS significantly reduced the incidence of POAF and attenuated inflammatory responses post-surgery. These findings suggest that LLVNS may serve as a therapeutic strategy to improve postoperative outcomes in cardiac surgery patients by modulating autonomic function and reducing inflammation.

This once again shows that self-inducing sensory input reduces the spikes in the brain which in turn is collaborating much more effectively with other parts of the human body. **This is the same effect that we want as golfers – an effective collaboration between Sensory Input and Motor Output with the least amount of impact from the context of the shot.**

🔑 Key Takeaways

- Neurohacks are quick, sensory-based tools to calm the brain and reduce distracting thoughts during competition.
- The Vagus nerve triggers fight-or-flight; neurohacks help 'stand it down' when the threat is not real.
- Self-induced sensory actions—like slow breathing or touching fingers—can spike down brain activity in seconds.
- Different neurohacks are needed for Red vs Yellow brain states; don't overuse powerful ones.
- Spike-downs improve motor control by enhancing sensory input and calming mental chatter.
- Verbalizing visuals ('Talk with Eyes') is more powerful than silent visualization.
- Neurohacks are scientifically backed to lower stress and enhance performance — they belong in every athlete's toolkit.

What percentage of time during your round of golf are you thinking of past shots, technique or your score? That's the percentage you're robbing your brain (and body) of what you're fully capable of doing.

05 | TARGETS

How Targets Shape Execution

Try not to think of the game of golf as an 18-hole or two 9-hole or a swing/ball striking/short game competition. Instead, consider golf as a 15-minute competition (the total time spent hitting shots over 18 holes) and your ability to hold a target without distraction over that time.

As stated in the introduction, GOLF IS A TARGET SPORT. The objective of this game is to send the ball to a target. Those targets are located in the fairway of your selection, a spot on the green from where you want to putt to the hole, or in the hole where you want the putt to enter the hole.

Golf is not the only target sport. Here are a few other target sports athletes engage in:

- **Soccer**: Using legs to pass the ball to a teammate or kick the ball into the opposing team's goal
- **Basketball**: Using arms/hands to pass the ball to a teammate or to shoot the ball into the hoop
- **Football**: Throwing the football to receivers, aiming to complete passes and advance towards the end zone
- **Baseball**: Throwing the ball towards the strike zone, aiming to challenge the batter and achieve strikes (pitcher)

- **Ice Hockey**: Passing to teammates and shooting the puck into the opponent's net
- **Handball**: Passing to teammates and aiming to throw the ball past the goalkeeper into the net
- **Water Polo**: Passing to teammates and shooting the ball into the opposing net
- **Lacrosse**: Passing to teammates and shoot the ball into the goal
- **Rugby Fly-Half**: A key playmaker who often kicks the ball through the uprights for points or passes to set up tries
- **Field Hockey**: Passing to teammates and hitting the ball into the opposing team's goal
- **Archer**: A competitor in archery aims to shoot arrows precisely at the center of a target from set distances
- **Darts**: Throwing at a circular board, striving to hit specific high-scoring areas, notably the bullseye
- **Rifle Shooter**: Using a rifle to shoot projectiles at a target a given distance away; the goal is to hit the target's center
- **Bowling**: Rolling a heavy ball down a lane to knock down a set of pins

In all of these target sports, a desired precision is sought after. If the target is missed, it is also desired that the dispersion of the miss be as small as possible. A set of neuromuscular sequencing is required for these sports for ONLY two reasons:

1. Generate the right amount of force for carrying the ball to the target.
2. Generate some kind of movement of the ball on its journey to the target.

In golf, the force is how hard the ball is struck by the club, and the movement would be a trajectory or shot shape to the target.

A major claim I am making is that it is the target that creates in the human brain a scale of how far/close it is from where you are. This scale in turn creates in the brain the most natural neuromuscular sequencing for the amount of force and shot shape desired for that selected target.

So why is Golf the most difficult target sport?

There are four major reasons why Golf is the most difficult target sport:

1. Eyes are off the target at the start of a swing/stroke
2. Unique location for every shot (changing target for each shot)
3. Fast target image decay (new images constantly coming into brain)
4. Constant internal distractions

Let's explore the above from a neuroscience perspective.

NEUROSCIENCE OF TARGETS (Basis on claim)

1. Eyes are off the target at the start of a swing/stroke

If I were to ask you, how far you are from …

Well, right now you are probably thinking there's a typo and I did not finish that sentence. It is confusing to your brain.

If I were to then ask you, how far are you from New York City (NYC)? Instantly, from wherever you are, your brain is mapping out a line to NYC. Your brain is processing distance or drive time or flight duration and perhaps even other logistics like stops on the way. This is the power of a target in the brain.

A discovery in neuroscience that led to a Nobel Prize was that of Grid Neurons. In 2005, Norwegian neuroscientists May-Britt Moser and Edvard I. Moser discovered these cells while studying rats navigating open spaces. Grid cells are specialized neurons located in the brain's entorhinal cortex that activate in multiple areas enabling spatial navigation by creating an internal coordinate system. This is sometimes referred to as a Euclidean Map (Moser & Moser, 2005). Their research revealed that grid cells, along with hippocampal place cells, form a neural basis for spatial memory and navigation. In recognition of their groundbreaking work, the **Mosers, together with John O'Keefe — who had previously identified place cells — were awarded the 2014 Nobel Prize in Physiology or Medicine** for their discoveries of cells that constitute a positioning system in the brain.

For Golfers, this could be one of the most insightful studies to read. What makes golf different from all other precision/target sports and makes it the most difficult target sport of all? **A golfer's eyes are NOT on the target when initiating the neuromuscular sequence!** This means that a concerted effort has to be made by the golfer to pick the kind of targets that keep those grid neurons ACTIVE just before the initiation of the neuromuscular sequencing! Without eyes on the target, the Euclidean Map is necessary for muscle sequencing and application of force. If the target is not active in the brain just before initiating the golf swing/stroke (i.e., no map), it is very much like the first question I asked earlier about where you are without giving you a destination.

I make another major claim that the ability to recall a target (activated grid neurons) whilst not looking at the target is the most important skill in golf, especially for shots requiring precise neuromuscular sequence for force like putts inside 10 feet or so. I discuss this more in the next chapter.

Like all skills in golf, this is a skill that can be learned and should be practiced. Without a target in your brain, neuromuscular sequencing and force are vulnerable, especially if the context of the shot is high, where your brain is operating in Yellow or Red. Having activated grid neurons (target) is not a guarantee of a perfect shot, but it certainly is a guarantee of much smaller dispersion.

If you would like a quick experiment to prove the above, take three golf balls or any balls right now (wherever you are) and:

1. Find a spot about five feet away and throw the ball looking at that spot.
2. Find a different spot about five feet away and throw the ball at that spot with your eyes closed.
3. Find a different spot again about five feet away and throw the ball to that spot with your eyes closed; but this time, before you throw, take about 10 seconds, and find several attributes of that spot you feel you can recall. Now close your eyes, recall those attributes, and then throw the ball to that spot.

Typical results are:

1. Almost everyone hits the spot on the first attempt. Eyes are on the close target. Grid neurons are very active. No thought in the brain, just sensory (visual) input because the target is so close.
2. In the second scenario, most people come up short. Grid neurons are not as active (eyes are closed).
3. In the last scenario, most people are very close to the first scenario.

Scenario 2 is similar to asking, "how far are you from…?" but without specifying the destination. The collaboration between sensory input and motor sequence is compromised. Some type of neuromuscular disruption is highly likely.

In scenarios 1 and 3, "NYC" (i.e., the target/location) has been provided to the brain. Sensory input about the target with and without the eyes on that target has activated the grid neurons. This creates a scale which then organizes the right muscle sequencing to apply the right force to send the ball to the target.

2. Unique location for every shot (changing target for each shot)

Almost every shot on the golf course is in a unique geospatial location over 300+ acres of land. Almost all other target sports listed earlier in this chapter are confined to a specific and constant field size or small location. In these sports, like basketball, one can practice shooting from a location (spot on the court) and the basket will always be the same and similar distance from that location. Grid neurons are imprinted thousands of times and without looking, these athletes in these sports 'know' where they are. Not so in golf. Depending on the weather (sunshine, cloudy, windy, fall, spring, etc.) and where your ball ends up, the golfer is forced to take a target for that specific shot that is very unique to that moment. Putting is a particularly difficult target selection challenge because every putt is likely to have a unique path to travel. I discuss this in more detail in the next chapter.

It is my claim that the target selection should be the most important part of the golf shot. I argue that if a good target is not selected, the odds of a neuromuscular disruption increase. And no amount of technique can cure this missing input. A perfect golf swing or putting stroke are wonderful skills to have but without a target, the scale is lost (how far your brain thinks it is from the destination), and this will invariably spike the brain as it is aware of the desired outcome of a high-quality shot.

3. Fast target image decay (new images constantly coming into the brain)

Target Degradation is a term used in Visual Cortex. The retina is not the final destination of where an image (target) will live in the brain. The optic nerve carries images (targets) to the back of the brain to several 'screens' that are simply called the V1 Screen for the purposes of this book.

When you are watching a movie, note that the image on the screen is changing roughly every three seconds. Even if it is the same scene, camera angles are changing, backgrounds are changing, the music may also be changing. These constant changes are very intentional and designed to keep our attention as an audience. This is why scenes take so long to shoot as they have to be shot in so many different viewpoints and ultimately put together in editing post filming to create the most compelling sequence to engage the audience.

The V1 Screen is also constantly changing about three times in one second according to some studies (Leopold & Logothetis, 1998). This is very intentional also and for the purpose of survival, arguably an important factory setting design. Our eyes need to constantly scan the environment around us to give input to identify and divert any possible danger or threats. But this is not good for golf! When our heads make that final movement away from the target down to the ball and club head, the target selected begins its natural decay process. Grid neurons are being deactivated almost instantly as we: (1) look away from target, and (2) have new images showing up on that V1 screen (ball, club head, feet, ground, etc.). Picking high quality targets that take longer to decay is a skill that can be learned and practiced.

4. Constant internal distractions

Our own brains are distracting us every three seconds! This was discussed in earlier chapters. In other words, the speed of the decay of the target on the V1 screen is being accelerated with those pesky distractions carrying spiking electricity. This now means that the target is lost, resulting in neuromuscular sequence disruption!

Is there any good news about the brain and targets? Yes! But we have to understand what we are trying to fix and now you know!

There are skills to taking high quality targets (target selection) and WHEN to take them that can activate and amplify grid neurons so that their decay is slowed long enough to have it active at the start of your backswing/stroke.

Debunking the Myth of Small Target Small Miss

My extensive research has found no studies to support this anecdotal and seemingly wide-held belief. I believe there might be a placebo effect.

I have studied the brain during target selection, and it is not the size of the target that determines the quality of the target. **A high-quality target for golfers is a target that can be easily recalled when the eyes are no longer on it.** Some small targets are actually very bad in the sense that because they are small, they are lost instantly. Other small targets are actually very good. What is the reason for this?

CONTRAST

The most important attribute of a high-quality target is CONTRAST. The brain loves contrast. It stands out more from the norm. Yes, some contrasts presented on the 300+ acre golf course are small and others are big. Key elements in contrast are COLOR and SHAPE.

A green blade of grass an inch short of the hole is a target for a putt. A better target might be a brown or white grass blade very nearby. Green on Green is not a contrast. Brown or White on Green is a contrast.

On approach shots, a spot on the green to land the ball is a target. A better target might be the contour on the green where it changes color based on slope or grain or sunshine.

On a Tee shot, a spot in the fairway is a target, but way above that spot in the tree line background of the hole is a V-shape between two trees near each other. The V-shape coupled with the green of the tree lines against the blue sky is a far superior image on the V1 screen and higher quality target.

Take a look at the following image (Figure 7). Look at it carefully and see if you can determine which circle in the middle is bigger?

Figure 7.

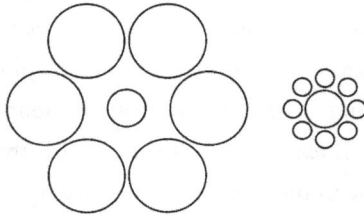

Picking Targets

Most people will pick the one on the right. The correct answer is that they are both the same size. This illusion created by scientists (*Tichner's Circle*) drives home the point of contrast. The middle circle on the right appears bigger because of the contrast created by the small circles around it.

The golf course is actually visually amazing if you flip the script. Sure, it is over 300+ acres, but the search of contrasting targets is itself a neurohack. Eyes looking around the hole for a high-quality target is high quality sensory input. Eyes looking for a high-quality target on approach shots on or above green is high quality sensory input. Eyes looking for trees or tree lines from Tee boxes is high quality sensory input. Adding to all this effort, the search for colors and shapes is an even more powerful neurohack.

Recall from Chapter 3:

High Quality Sensory Input = High Quality Motor Output.

The search for high quality targets not only amplifies the activation of grid neurons, but also lowers the EEG; it is a powerful combo of good use of time in your pre-shot routine for all golf shots.

WHEN to take targets?

This may seem like a silly question but there is neuroscience data supporting that EARLY selection is better. By early selection, I mean early in your pre-shot routine.

Early target selection has been shown to significantly enhance retention and decision-making in neuroscience studies. Research indicates that when monitoring multiple information sources, the human brain employs discrete, early target selection signals that modulate the onset and rate of neural evidence accumulation (Loughnane et al., 2016). These signals influence both the timing and accuracy of perceptual reports. In uncertain environments, such as when evidence appears unpredictably in time and space, early target selection helps the brain effectively process relevant information (Loughnane et al.). This mechanism is particularly important in real-world scenarios where we must continuously monitor our surroundings for important cues (Loughnane et al.). Additionally, studies have found that attention expedites target selection by prioritizing the neural processing of relevant stimuli (Bartsch et al., 2021).

Finding high quality targets as early as possible in your routine (especially if you are waiting for your turn to hit) is highly recommended. Think of coats of paint you are applying to a wall in your home. The more coats of paint are applied, the thicker and richer the paint and its color will stick to the wall. One coat of paint may fade much faster than multiple coats of paint.

In the brain, as discussed before, the 'wall' in the above paint analogy is the V1 Screen. The same screen where images are decaying very quickly (3X per second!). Early selection allows for more looks at the target, and more looks from different angles, creating an even more powerful grid neuron community that will stay active longer (it takes a village!!).

Conversely, late target selection is not recommended. Picking a target in the last 10 seconds of your routine (before you initiate your backswing/stroke) is basically 'just

1 coat of paint' and unless it has a spectacular contrast of color and shape, it will decay on the V1 screen instantly.

The Power of the LAST LOOK

The final piece of the puzzle is the power of the last look. I define the last look at the target as the last look before initiating backswing/stroke. This typically happens after you are fully set up to hit the golf shot over the ball. There is confirmation that the ball is in the right place in the stance and all other preparation boxes are checked off. This is when I recommend a 'final coat of paint' – a gentle and high-quality stare at the target recalling all the contrasting attributes you selected earlier. In my measurements, I consistently found this final image on the V1 screen to be one of the highest quality sensory inputs resulting in very high-quality motor output.

♀ Key Takeaways

- Golf is a target sport, and target selection drives motor accuracy and shot quality.
- Grid neurons activate spatial awareness; without a target, your brain lacks a destination to calibrate force.
- Golf is harder than other target sports because you don't look at the target while executing the shot.
- High-contrast targets (shape, color) are more memorable and effective than small or vague ones.
- Early target selection strengthens memory and reduces visual decay on the brain's 'screen' (V1).
- The brain naturally distracts every three seconds — reinforcing target images helps override this decay.
- A purposeful 'last look' anchors the target image and improves swing/stroke precision.

You are the sole author of the narrative of your poor shots. No one is wirelessly telling you what to tell yourself. Be the kind of author that, no matter the tragedy, the power of the lesson is always the Headline.

06 | PUTTING

Precision, Pressure, And Brain Spikes

> *You don't choose your first thought, but you can choose your last thought before stroke. You don't choose to think about the missed putt on the last hole, but you can choose to think about the blade of grass over which the ball will enter the hole.*

We are now getting into the heart of this book. I consider myself an Accidental Putting Coach. This was never a goal of mine. As my research evolved and I began to see the dramatic impact it was having on the mental state of golfers and on putting, I realized I had stumbled on, possibly, new knowledge and skills.

From a brain scanning perspective (research), putting is one of the easiest to study, especially inside 15 feet. Here are the reasons why:

1. The target is very close.
2. The neuromuscular sequence is one that requires few motor functions (not a violent or fast pattern).
3. The force required to be generated is low.
4. Because the target is small (Cup), the precision required of all of the above is very high.
5. Results are very quickly tracked (was made or not).

It was, therefore, easier to measure EEG by standing just a few feet away, pre, during and post putt.

Full shots (off the Tee or approach shots from the fairway) are farther away and their pin-point accuracy is not a premium (missing the center of the fairway by two yards is not a problem) like a putt would be.

In the opening chapters, I shared several key points that, at this point in the book, are worth revisiting given the knowledge you now have based on the previous chapters.

Here are the earlier points as it relates to this chapter on putting:

1. During the process of conducting 18,000 EEG scans, many unexpected insights were discovered.

2. One major insight is the argument that golf is the most difficult target sport. This is due to the unique challenge of aiming at a target while looking down at the ball rather than the target itself.

3. Unlike other target sports like football, soccer, and basketball, where athletes maintain visual contact with their target, golfers must rely heavily on memory and spatial awareness. This disconnect creates a major visual and cognitive challenge unique to golf.

4. Golf also differs in the variability of its playing field — 18 different holes over hundreds of acres — whereas other sports are played on a single, consistent field. This variation increases reliance on target selection and mental mapping in golf.

5. Golfers' visual cortex is saturated with immediate visual input — putter head, ball, feet — but not the actual target. This leads to difficulty in recalling and executing accurate shots because the target is degraded in the brain's V1 screen.

6. Poor shots often stem not from physical error but from neural confusion between the visual and motor cortices. Without an image of the target in your V1 screen, the brain sends uncertain instructions, resulting in mis-executed putts.

7. EEG scans revealed a surprising and consistent increase in brain electricity as players moved from tee to green towards the skill of putting. Initially dismissed as device error, this pattern of *pressure building on the green* proved

to be a reliable indicator of spikes and even major surges of electricity if the context is high.

8. The brain spikes on the green for three reasons: the score is about to be finalized, the margin for error is smallest, and the required motor movement is extremely precise. Each of these factors significantly raises the stakes for the golfer.

9. Putting is unique in requiring a gentle, highly controlled stroke on the smoothest part of the course. Despite this simplicity, the higher inherent EEG mental state often disrupts the low-frequency brain activity needed for precision.

10. I believe most putts inside 10 feet are makeable, and the 40% PGA Tour average is the most opportunistic area of improvement towards score. The main culprit is not physical inability, but excessive mental interference that elevates brain activity and disrupts the putting stroke.

NEURO-BASED PUTTING TIPS

1. Taking Vs Holding Targets

I see golfers of all skill levels spending a reasonably acceptable amount of time TAKING the target. Some of the more common green reading tasks include:

- Determining breaks based on contours
- Determining grain of grass
- Determining starting lines
- Determining impact of wind
- Walking to many spots to assess the above data
- Picking a break point
- Picking a target

All of this very necessary information is being captured by the eyes. Sensory input from the eyes is being cognitively processed to make a decision. This is **TAKING** the target. But what is the value of this information if it is lost just before or during your putting stroke? Should the most important skill not be to have this information in your brain while not looking at the target? If your brain is not **HOLDING** the target in your brain, especially just before initiating the putting stroke, what do you think is the quality of motor output without this target sensory input? There is a very high probability that some form of neuromuscular disruption is going to occur, as discussed in previous chapters.

Here is an exercise I strongly encourage you to do. In just a few seconds, close your eyes and describe your childhood bedroom. Describe the furniture, decorations, paint, and as many attributes as you can recall. Stop after about 30 seconds. Please do this now.

If you are skipping this exercise, I again encourage you not to skip it but give it a try. It's just 30 seconds! If you have done it, great! Now read on.

I want to again make a claim that what you just did is the most important skill in both putting and golf. How so?

1. Unless you're a junior currently living in your home, you just described something you have not seen in years and maybe decades.
2. In putting, the complementary skills to TAKING the target described above is to HOLD the target before and during your putting stroke.
3. If you can describe something that your eyes are not currently on, that you have not seen in years, your childhood bedroom, then you can certainly describe a putting target that you just had your eyes on a few seconds earlier.

(Note: the same requirement of holding targets applies to all golf shots for the one powerful reason that your eyes are not on the target when executing motor function).

Recall that all visual input is decaying in the brain at an astonishing speed (3x per second) because of constant new images being captured by the eyes. This coupled with the high frequency of the hippocampal context of the putt as well as the natural increase on EEG on all greens on the golf course means that without a concerted effort to HOLD the target, the value of TAKING the target is lost. I see almost a 95% to 5% ratio in most golfers in terms of effort being made on taking the target (95%) versus holding the target (5%). My recommendation is not a 50-50 split but rather a sequence split. Take a look at the following image (Figure 8):

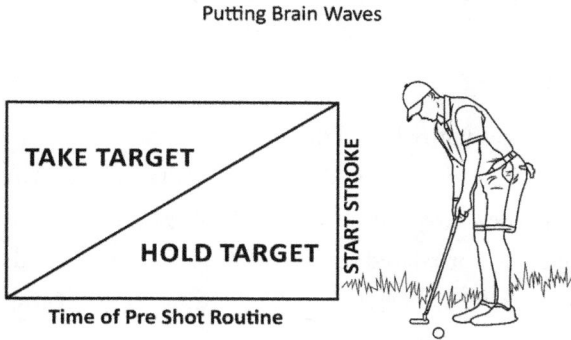

Figure 8.

Putting Brain Waves

TAKE TARGET

HOLD TARGET

START STROKE

Time of Pre Shot Routine

Let's assume your pre-shot routing is 60 seconds long. My suggestion is to use the first 30 seconds for all the green reading tasks (Cognitive Function) listed earlier (Taking Target) and the latter for sensory function (Target Holding). Once the 'math' has been done (Taking Target), it is now about spiking down any distractions and activating the grid neurons (Targets).

Taking the target is a visual sensory input taken with the eyes largely landing on the retina and quickly processed with context. Holding the target is that visual input active in the V1 Screen in the back of the brain without context – the target is just a target.

2. Early Target Selection

As discussed in Chapter 5, selecting targets early allows for additional coats of paint on the V1 screen, thereby increasing the likelihood of maintaining focus on targets. This process keeps grid neurons activated, which creates a sense of scale (distance from the target). Consequently, this enables a natural and instinctive stroke that generates the precise amount of force needed to hit the ball towards the selected target.

Even in the initial 30 seconds of cognitive functions of green reading, it is recommended that you begin to select the target early, especially putts inside 12 feet, and use the cognitive function to validate or adjust that initial target.

3. High Quality Putting Targets

The quality of the target you select is directly related to the decay rate of the target on your V1 Screen (holding target). High quality targets are easier to hold. CONTRAST is the key attribute of a high-quality target, not size. As discussed earlier, a small target is not related to a good target. There is no data that supports this seemingly universally held belief. A contrasting target, irrespective of size, is very high quality and the research supports this.

Every putt on the golf course is going to be a unique putt because every green is different, every hole location is different and where your ball is from the hole will be different. So, the skill to learn to take all kinds of targets that might be available on each putt is very important, especially for makeable putts. You are severely handicapping yourself by being exclusively a "die" putter or a "firm" putter. **Be a TARGET PUTTER!**

Here are just some examples of putting targets. In each one, a contrast of color or shape should be observable:

- Different color of grass blades
- Shape of cup
- Color/Shape of any imperfections around cup
- Color/Shape of imperfections inside cup
- Pitch mark or other anomalies near cup
- Colors/Shapes back of cup
- Entry point spots
- Shadows (leave the pin in if the shadow presents the entry point target)
- Sound of ball dropping
- Sound of ball at back of cup
- Motion (video) of ball traveling over several spots into hole

What all of these have in common is very high-quality sensory input that is directly visual. If good targets are not available, other sensory input can be used to amplify the desired visual target.

4. Pick Targets From The Hole Back

Yet another accidental discovery was made while processing WHERE the best targets should be selected from. I am well aware that there is a large school of thought that emphasizes start lines. Or Aim Point that creates a hypothetical target. I want to claim that start lines and Aim Point serve the important task of alignment, but alignment is not the target. A target is the final destination, it is exclusively what activates the grid neurons.

In full golf shots off the Tee box or on approach shots, golfers need some kind of alignment information. The most common one is to pick a spot just in front of your ball and set up your stance parallel to that spot. That spot is NOT your target. The target is where you want the ball to finish. The spot in front of your ball is the start line and a very useful step in executing the shot.

Putting is no different. I see too many golfers being overly focused on their start lines. Some have even said after missing a putt, "but I started it on the line." I am baffled by this consolation statement.

In every target sport I have studied, final destination targets are dominating in the brains of athletes when precision is achieved. A basketball player when shooting is thinking only of where the ball is going to enter the basket. A baseball pitcher when pitching is thinking only of where in the strike zone he wants to ball to finish. A soccer player when kicking is thinking of where the ball needs to end, whether passing to a teammate or target a post in the goal. An archer shooting an arrow is amplifying the specific color of the board where she wants the arrow to hit. None of them are thinking of where they start.

Starting lines and any target that does not involve the hole will activate the wrong grid neurons. The search for high quality putting targets must start at the hole and be around the hole. This is the final destination that creates a grid in the brain for the scale and force required to apply to the ball. A contrasting target in the hole, on the edge of it or within inches of the hole is a gift to your brain!

There are some breaking putts of course. In these cases, golfers tend to focus on the point of where the putt will break. This is fine so long as a connection is drawn from that break point to the hole.

5. Putting Routine Vs Putting Process

One of the many accidental discoveries made in my functional EEG scans was the high amount of mind wandering during the putting pre-shot routine. I am still surprised when I follow a golfer through their putting routine and see spikes (mind is not focused, thinking about something else). I have tried to see where the most common distractions occurred and if there were any themes. I could not find any specific points that were common, but I did find that when the brain finds a target, especially early in the routine, mind wandering increases if the subsequent tasks are meaningless and being done for the sake of doing the tasks versus doing them to gain additional valuable information.

I am aware that many in the golf community will again dispute this claim, but I have data that supports that doing any task of no value increases mind wandering (distractions). Identical putting routines, done over and over again for all putts and always the same, do not in fact support the widely held belief that routines have a 'calming' effect or a beneficial effect. Once the brain has achieved its objective, green reading and target selection, any task beyond that is not necessary and the brain is fully aware it is doing meaningless tasks if the objectives are met.

Take for example a 1-foot putt. Would you follow your normal full putting routine? Likely not. Why not? I argue because the target is quickly selected and clear (eyes are fully on the ball and target). After achieving all the necessary information about the putt, going through a full routine is meaningless after this point. The mind will begin to distract itself since self-distraction is the default factory setting of the brain and is already at an all-time high (Chapter 2). I have seen this play out countless times in my scans and one of the more valuable skills I have taught golfers is the awareness (measured in real time) of when in their routines they are spiking. **These spikes seem to be consistently correlated to points when the brain is not engaged in a meaningful task.**

Stating the obvious, not all putts require the same amount of due diligence as every putt you have on the course will be different.

Instead, I recommend a Putting Process. It is simple:

1. Find a good target (do what is required to find it – Green Reading and Target Selection)
2. Shift tasks to holding the target
3. The confirmation of the target in your brain (V1 screen) should initiate your stroke

The above PROCESS should not be task or time dependent. If it takes five seconds to do the above (1-foot putt), so be it. If it takes 60 seconds to do the above (more complex putt), so be it. This is an ATHLETIC way to putt. In reactionary sports, athletes are quickly processing what an opponent is doing or where the ball is going and their body responds with the appropriate motor pattern. If you are playing basketball and try to score a basket, your eyes are going to find a spot to shoot from where there is no defender or if there is one, to move to another spot away from that defender. The athlete is reacting to visual sensory input and instinctively moves (motor movement) to the best place to achieve the goal. Putting is similar except the target is not moving and no one is playing defense BUT the brain still wants and needs something to react to – that is HOLDING the target when the eyes are not on target. A good process that can change as needed is a better approach than a predetermined non-flexible routine.

6. One Look vs Many Looks

When over the ball, I have studied the difference between many looks at the hole versus fewer. I recommend fewer (one or two) looks where each is longer, and each is performing quality target confirmation tasks. More and quicker looks are not recommended. The latter, like practice strokes, is a motor movement. Your head has to turn to the hole as well as your eyes. This is not happening by accident – it is being coordinated by the brain. The more of these motor movements your brain must coordinate, the more competition there is in the brain for high quality sensory input. As a golfer, you will have to experiment with this on your own to find how many looks work for you but decide which looks are giving your retina an image versus giving your V1 Screen an image. Over the ball, we want more images on the V1 screen which will help hold the target once your eyes are no longer on the target. The retina is not where targets will be retrieved—quick looks seem to target the retina just because they are so quick and valuable time is clicking away where targets on the V1 screen are decaying quickly.

7. Eliminate Practice Strokes Over the Ball

Another accidental discovery was made when I observed golfers over the putt in the precious seconds before initiating the putting stroke. I repeatedly saw spikes. Once all the pre-work is completed and a target is selected, most golfers take their practice strokes when they are over the ball. There are many versions of this. Some have one practice, and others have more. Some look down at the ball while doing it, others look at the hole. Some are not thinking about anything, and others have a putting technical thought they want to remind themselves of.

I view the last 5-10 seconds as the most sacred time of the process. In this period, any task that is non-sensory and not adding a 'coat of target paint' on the V1 cortex, is a task that results in some level of spike.

A practice stroke is a motor movement that has to be coordinated by your brain. Your brain has to instruct your arms and hands to take the putter back to some point, from there return it to another point (follow through) and then stop. Your arms and hands are not doing this on their own. This motor coordination is robbery from sensory input. It is the wrong time (seconds before initiating stroke) and place (over the ball) to 'practice' any motor movement. In addition, it is not really a practice stroke, is it? You're not actually hitting a ball – you're hitting air. You're not hitting to a target, you're just moving the putter. So, it is not a true simulation of what you're about to do.

If you want to have the practice stroke to feel something or reinforce a technical thought, I recommend you do it much earlier in the process and not after you have walked over to the ball.

For the die-hard practice strokes golfers, there is one very minor exception I did find in practice strokes over the ball. Keep eyes on the target and then do a practice stroke intensely, sensing movement of the ball towards that target. I saw fewer and lower grade spikes in this scenario. This is largely because the practice stroke is serving a very powerful task of confirming high quality sensory input of the target on the V1 screen. In general, I recommend that this can be done without any motor movement at all. The golfer's full attention on those last 5-10 seconds before stroke must be a clear image of the target in the brain. The brain is already very well aware it is about to perform a motor function requiring a precise sequence. Success of this sequence is highest when the target dominates the brain since the grid neurons are activated only by a target and a perfect grid/scale is created.

8. Force To Target (Not Line & Speed)

I am aware that the conventional wisdom is that putting is about line and speed. I am also aware of the debate of which is more important. I want to make a claim that the terminology, however well-intentioned, is incorrect. The brain seems to respond to a motor movement with commands that trigger the desired motor movement. Yell "JUMP" at someone and they are likely to jump, not do a dance. Both are motor movements, with the former matching the desired outcome. A coach yelling "SHOOT" at his basketball player is likely resulting in that player to shoot and not pass the ball.

Neither line nor speed are commands. Line is an analysis (path of the ball), and speed is the result of force being applied to the ball the motor movement.

I recommend golfers use the terms FORCE TO TARGET. The brain should be asking itself: *What force do I need to apply to this ball to send it there?* This combo of a command (Force) and target is a better mental framework. Once understood, I have seen consistently lower levels of EEG in the brain.

9. Repurpose Your Putting Wait Times

Imagine playing in your regular foursome and each of you shoot 75. If you watch all your shots, and while you're waiting to hit, you watch the routines and shots of your three playing partners, that is 300 shots that your brain has processed. In my opinion, that is 225 more shots than necessary that your brain had to process—a needless task! There's a massive difference to a hard-working brain processing 75 shots vs processing 300 shots!

Another claim I am making is that most golfers are giving their brains useless and garbage input while waiting for their turn to putt. What is the value to your brain of watching others putt? Unless it is the identical putt you have or on a similar location, the input of others putting should be repurposed to perform all the valuable tasks that is required for when it is your turn to putt.

I have discussed distractions and context as spiking the brain. If your putt is high context, and we already know golfer's EEG is higher on all greens, why not apply some neurohacks to lower the EEG? Why not start to select targets early? Why not stand in a position (since you have to be still on the putting green while others are putting) where you can have the best visual input to your putt? Why not start early in finding possible options of contrasting holdable targets? I call this Target Scanning, and it is a much better set of valuable input for the task of any precision motor sequencing.

You can see that by repurposing wait times on the greens, by replacing useless input with useful input, you are preparing yourself much better for a motor sequence that requires precision. **The more Brain Green you are on the green, the more you enhance the probability of achieving that precision!**

10. Address Your Putting Bully

Your #1 competitor while putting will not be green reading or target taking/holding: it will be the most recent memory of a missed similar putt. If on hole 12, for example, you have a 6-foot right to left putt, your brain will do its job (factory setting) and recall the last right to left putt that you missed whenever it happened previously. It will not recall all the right to left putts you made earlier or in years of practice.

This design of the brain is actually quite necessary for survival. If a lion ate your son in the Serengeti thousands of years ago, then the next time you hear, smell, or see a lion, your military systems need to get into high gear and immediately protect yourself and others. It is important to recall the trauma to make adjustments to not let it happen again. Your true competition is the bully of your previous missed similar putt. If that bully is replaying in your brain, you are spiking. You will not be able to hold the target, and a neuromuscular disruption is highly likely.

72

My recommendation is very counter intuitive and likely to draw ridicule amongst experts. I recommend if you have a putt where you recently missed a similar one, then you proactively recall that putt while walking to green, in your wait times or very early in your routine and make an effort to dilute it by forcing yourself to think of any good recent putt you can recall. Intentionally extracting that memory will prevent it from that memory deciding on its own when it will show up and it will usually show up to your conscious awareness while over the ball or worse, during your stroke. Why would anyone recommend that you recall a negative experience? Is this not the opposite of "staying positive" and having confidence? I did not design the brain, but I can tell you that the polarity of a recent negative experience is a very high spike. It is a set of charged neurons ready to help you. The neurobiology and neurochemistry design of the brain does not distinguish between the lion eating your son and the previous missed similar putt. Both were trauma where excited neurons were activated.

🔑 Key Takeaways

- Putting requires precise neuromuscular control and is the most mentally demanding part of the game.
- EEG scans show golfers' brains spike most on the green — due to precision demands and high emotional stakes.
- Most golfers take targets well, but fail to hold them during execution, causing disruption in motor output.
- High-quality targets have strong contrasts, and should be selected early in the routine, then held in memory.
- Replacing rigid routines with flexible, sensory-based putting processes reduces mind-wandering and enhances performance.
- Practice strokes over the ball add unnecessary brain load; target recall should dominate final seconds before stroke.
- Your brain stores missed putts vividly — acknowledge and overwrite these memories early with positive ones to avoid performance disruption.

The cost of executing a high-quality putt should not include the price of your last poor similar putt.

07 | PRACTICE

Train for Game-Time Recall

Golf swings, chipping, and putting strokes are ruined more by your own brain noise than by lack of skill.

I have found practice to be one of the more fascinating areas to explore where neuroscience can make a significant impact. I began to study practice in several sports, especially after COVID when coaches and athletes started to *en masse* call me and state that the correlation between practice and game-time performance was getting lower and almost non-existent. This is very troubling – to think that practice is not transferring over to competition. I had a very experienced National Championship head coach tell me that she no longer knew which team would show up on the field. It used to be, she said, that for the most part good practices translated to good games, but not anymore. It wasn't until warm-ups that she had a good gauge of where her athletes were and how they would perform. At this point though, adjustment options are very limited. So, I studied what exactly practice is, which seems like a silly concept at first pass.

During a round of golf, where is the knowledge of what decision to make and the golf shot to hit coming from? No one is wirelessly transferring that information to you, and you are not on your phone Googling how to hit a shot. Well, again, it sounds silly, but information is coming from an inventory in a storage facility that is your brain. ACCESS to the full inventory of your knowledge and skills during your round is key.

As shared in Chapter 3, access along with dilution of sensory input is compromised if the brain is not around 10 Hz. This is where the in-the-moment neurohacks can help spike down the electricity surges from distractions or high context shots. But practice is where inventory is created.

The claim here is that the sole purpose of practice is to create a retrievable game-time inventory.

Similar to the concept of taking vs holding targets, if practice inventory is not intentionally stored to begin with, there is no inventory to access during the round.

I had a player call me after a poor first tournament round on a Thursday evening. He had been off the previous two weeks and had been practicing very hard and getting good results. He even said he had his best week practicing and felt very prepared going into the tournament. He stated: "*By the 3rd hole, I was playing the shots I had to hit and I never once thought about anything good I did from the 2 weeks of high-quality practice.*"

Clearly, practice was not retrievable to this golfer during the first round, not just from the previous two weeks, but also from a lifetime of playing and practicing hitting thousands of balls. What happened to the inventory from the two weeks of good practice?

There are three components to any knowledge retrievable process but specifically practice:

1. Practice
2. Effective Storage of practice (called ENCODING)
3. Retrieval during competition of specific inventory related to shot at hand

Coaches and athletes have incorrectly assumed that the process of practice itself guarantees steps 2 and 3. Based on Chapter 2, we now know that, more than ever, the inventory of life itself, with all the constant stimuli is at an all-time high. **There have never been people who have walked the surface of earth who have more daily stimuli (inventory) than us.** This is the cost of being human today.

The brain has a very limited daily storage space for inventory. There are now unprecedented levels of competition within the brain of what to store and discard.

Left to itself, it will regrettably prioritize inventory that is of higher frequency (negative) than lower more positive inventory because the former is more relevant to survival and simply put, more neurons are polarized (activated) with negative stimuli.

Take this simple example. Let's say you spend four hours on the range practicing. You have done several drills in several parts of your game, and it was amazing. You truly felt like you had accomplished the requirements of a good practice. Immediately after practice, you get a call from your significant other that they are breaking up with you. This is a major surprise to you that occurred subsequent to the great practice session. This terrible news from your significant other is new inventory for your brain to process, a massively higher frequency, and that evening virtually none of the shots you hit in your practice will be **ENCODED** (stored correctly) and, therefore, none of the practice will be retrieved in your next competitive round. I understand that in reality most of you are not going to get this kind of news right after a good practice so substitute break-up news with virtually any negative inventory you are going to consume on your phone and in your interactions with others from the moment you finish your practice to when you go to bed. I am arguing that each experience has a dilution impact on the value of the practice simply because it is a new inventory and it is inventory that came after your practice (layered on top of practice inventory).

In the next chapter, I discuss sleep. For now, note that research indicates that sleep plays a crucial role in memory encoding and consolidation. During sleep, particularly slow-wave sleep (SWS) and rapid eye movement (REM) sleep, the brain actively processes and stabilizes new information acquired during wakefulness. According to Born and Wilhelm (2012), SWS facilitates the transfer of newly encoded memories from the hippocampus to the neocortex for long-term storage. Additionally, REM sleep is associated with the integration and strengthening of emotional and procedural memories (Walker & Stickgold, 2006). Neuroimaging studies reveal reactivation of hippocampal patterns during sleep that mirror those seen during learning, supporting the idea that the brain rehearses and consolidates information overnight (Diekelmann & Born, 2010). These findings collectively demonstrate that sleep is not merely a passive state but an active period during which the brain encodes, consolidates, and enhances memory.

I want to claim that the most important hour of your practice is the hour before you sleep.

Since very little encoding (memory formation) is done during practice and largely done at night, it is important to move the practice inventory from earlier in the day back to the top of conscious inventory by actively replaying your practice. Doing so an hour before sleep also ensures that no new inventory will overlay your replay since you are imminently going to sleep.

Engram Sparsity is the principle suggesting that only a limited number of memories (Engrams) can be stored each day (Richards & Frankland, 2017). Studies using optogenetics have shown that reactivating just these sparse engram cells can trigger full memory retrieval (Liu et al., 2012). Encoding is thus a core principle in how the brain stores and protects long-term memories.

To be clear, I am not suggesting that practice is not important. It is very important to keep learning and building the overall inventory. I am suggesting that practice without encoding has become more and more useless in the constantly stimulated world we now live in. This largely explains what those coaches and athletes have been experiencing with unpredictable and inconsistent performances. They are doing practice as they always have, when cognitive stimulation was not so high, and sleep was not the global pandemic it is now.

Here are several neuroscience-based techniques to help you practice and encode the practice so that game-time retrieval is enhanced.

1. Record Your Key Learnings Immediately After Practice

ENCODING: I advise coaches and athletes that whatever time has been allocated to practice and whatever task is being performed in practice, that the last 15 minutes be fully dedicated to some way of recording the key elements of the practice. I strongly recommend self-videos where you can record yourself capturing the highlights and key learnings. Writing in a notebook or on your notes app in your phone are acceptable alternatives. Then these recordings should be reviewed intensely in that last hour before sleep. Try to relive the practice in your mind with your eyes closed after watching your videos or reading your notes. Perhaps it was something you found on the range with a certain club, or short game area.

2. Eliminate Spikes One hour Post Practice

Whenever possible, manage your time for the one hour post-practice. This is the second most important hour of the day outside the hour before bed. This is not the time to self-induce spikes. There's a reason I used the example of the breakup earlier. It was to underscore the power of negative (spikes) inventory post practice. One hour post-practice is not the time to go to social media and consume inventory that will spike you or talk to someone who will spike you or to engage in activities that will spike you. I do understand the realities of life's obligations and responsibilities, however. Plan your day so that if there are high-charged activities that have to be done, they are done before practice or after an hour of finishing practice.

3. Hormesis

Memory formation (encoding during practice) can be enhanced despite the challenges I have already discussed. During practice, encoding is rare, but it can serve the indirect purpose of helping you make better selfie videos and inventory to record. This approach ensures that the hour before sleep practice is significantly optimized.

Hormesis is good stress – which may appear contradictory. Hormesis, the biological phenomenon where low-dose stressors enhance cellular function and resilience, has been shown to positively influence memory consolidation. Mild stressors such as intermittent fasting, exercise, and cognitive challenges activate adaptive cellular responses that support brain plasticity and memory formation. According to Calabrese and Mattson (2017), hormetic stress activates signaling pathways, such as those involving brain-derived neurotrophic factor (BDNF), which promote synaptic growth and strengthen neural circuits involved in memory. These findings suggest that hormetic stressors prime the brain for improved cognitive performance by promoting neuroplasticity and enhancing the physiological mechanisms that underlie memory consolidation.

Golf practice is a lonely practice. Coaches are rarely present and there are no teammates to pass the ball to or to play defense for you. So how can you introduce Hormesis into golf practice?

1. Make every three shots you hit, no matter the shot or club in hand, a "game-time" shot, not a practice. How do you play shots when in competition? What are attributes of in-competition shots?

    a. There is one ball to hit
    b. The shot has high frequency context
    c. There is a specific target, yardage, shot shape, etc.
    d. There is a full pre-shot routine
    e. There is a full post-shot evaluation
    f. An adjustment is made if necessary

2. Limit practice time on each part of the game to a maximum of 20 minutes. There is a finite attention span in the brain especially with repetitive tasks. If you have only one hour of practice, you are better of practicing three different parts of the game (e.g., Putting, Wedges, Woods) than to spend the hour on only one part. Each new 20-minute session is a new beginning, which enhances attention, which in turn enhances encoding.

3. Take 5–10-minute full breaks every 20-30 minutes. A full break means completely detaching from golf. Call a friend or listen to music or take a nap with your eyes closed. This cognitive and sensory temporary detachment creates an even more powerful fresh start of high attention when you start after the break. Do not use this break to go on social media or consume high frequency stimuli – this is not a break!

4. If you practice playing on the course, play at least one shot per hole with a club you would otherwise not use in that situation. Force your brain to find inventory of something similar or make the right adjustment to execute the shot.

Kobe Bryant often emphasized the importance of making practice harder than the game. In interviews, he shared how he would take thousands of shots in practice, simulating game-like pressure and fatigue. He believed that if he trained with the same intensity and focus as a real game, then in actual competition, the shots would feel routine. One famous story recalls Kobe arriving at the gym at 4 a.m., practicing until others showed up hours later. He wanted to simulate fourth quarter fatigue when practicing with them!

4. Tournament Week Reactivation

Each morning and evening of the days leading up to your competitive round, and each night of your competitive round, is an amazing time to rewatch the library of videos from your practice. Again, **I make the claim that the sole purpose of practice is to create a game-time retrievable inventory.** Well, it's game-time week. Watching the recordings from all your practice, maybe a few each morning and evening, will propel this very necessary inventory to more retrievable status when you are actually playing. You will be amazed at how, when you are playing well, your brain will randomly think of good shots or similar circumstances you were in where you executed a positive shot or quickly remember an adjustment to make in your swing or putting!

♥ Key Takeaways

- The goal of practice is to create retrievable memories for game-time use — not just repetition or mechanical improvement.
- Memory encoding doesn't happen during practice — it happens later, especially during the hour before sleep.
- Without deliberate encoding, good practice is overwritten by post-practice distractions and emotional spikes.
- Use video/self-recording post-practice to summarize key takeaways; review them before bed to aid memory storage.
- Inject 'good stress' (hormesis) in practice — simulate game-like conditions, vary tasks, and increase focus.
- Take full cognitive breaks during practice and rotate areas of focus every 20 minutes to boost attention.
- Reactivate stored practice by reviewing your notes/videos before competition to bring inventory top-of-mind.

Your brain is the only place where you can remember something important and instantly become stronger than you are. And it's also the only place where you can forget something and become weaker than you are.

08 | SLEEP

Overnight Encoding for Peak Play

In the movie Gladiator, Maximus is told "win the crowd & you win your freedom." In neuroscience, if you can win the crowd in your head (control the monologues), you will win the freedom to be your best version, especially when it counts.

Of ALL the things you can do to get to 10 Hz and enhance your performance on the golf course, none is more important than sleep. Our understanding of sleep has dramatically changed just in the last couple of decades. We never really studied it because well, what is there to study – you are sleeping. We all figured the body was tired and needed rest.

It turns out the brain is performing very critical functions to prepare for the next day. If sleep is compromised, it can affect performance, especially if the goal is to perform at a high-level in golf.

The brain - though weighing less than 5 pounds - consumes about 20% at rest of all the energy of the body (metabolic resting rate). This increases with higher levels of cognitive function. The brain is soft tissue, no copper wiring is in it. This soft tissue generates waste and needs repair each day. This is a major purpose of sleep. During sleep, it is essential for the body to be motionless and free of sensory input - which is why sleep occurs while laying still in a horizontal position.

I have come to believe that no single behavior influences an athlete's next-day performance more than sleep. Not mindset. Not nutrition. Not even practice. Over the years, I've had athletes call me in full-blown confusion the morning of competition: "I don't know what's wrong. I had a great week, I feel prepared, but I just can't access it." **Access.** There's that word again. The common thread in these conversations? A terrible night of sleep the night before.

Sleep is not rest. It is not shutting off. It is not even recovery in the passive sense of the word. It is an active neurological reconfiguration process — one that determines whether the skills you built in practice are available to you in competition. One that determines whether your brain can enter that critical 10 Hz zone when it matters most. Sleep, in fact, may be the single most important encoding event of the day.

Why is Sleep the new Silent Pandemic?

For reasons discussed in Chapter 2, the volume and intensity of the constant stimuli consumption by the brain is at levels never before experienced by any generation of humans that have ever lived. **Each human day has become a mental marathon, and it is within this marathon that a round of golf is being played.** The only meaningful time the brain has to process all this inventory is during sleep.

Take a look at the following image (Figure 9) of people living in two identical homes that have a street in front. The first has car traffic all night long on the street, creating noise. The other has no car traffic, and so no noise. Which family would you guess will sleep better? Clearly the one with no street traffic.

Substitute the cars and traffic with stimuli you have consumed all day long. The cars are thoughts that your brain is processing. Negative thoughts/stimuli - because their polarity is so much higher - will tend to dominate your brain both just before and during your sleep, spiking you (waking you up).

Figure 9.

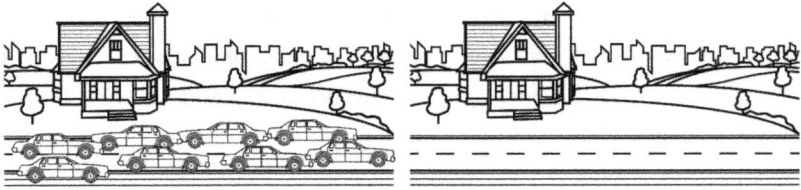

SLEEP: Underrated for Productivity

The modern athlete faces more sleep threats than any generation before them. Late-night screen time. Travel schedules. Pressure. Stimulation. Caffeine. Spikes. These are not small disruptions. They are performance-killers. And when you begin to understand what the brain actually does during sleep, especially in the stages of SWS and REM, you begin to see just how much is at stake.

Sleep is not one big thing. It is a sequence of biological functions that allows the brain to perform 10 essential operations that directly correlate with competitive performance.

Here are 10 core functions of the brain during sleep:

1. **Memory Consolidation (Hippocampal-to-Neocortical Transfer):**
    The brain does not store memories during learning — it stores them during sleep. Newly acquired knowledge (whether it's a swing change or a tactical insight) is initially encoded in the hippocampus. But it is fragile. Only during SWS does this memory get transferred to the neocortex for long-term storage. This is how temporary learning becomes durable knowledge.

2. **Emotional Regulation:**
    REM sleep plays a vital role in recalibrating the brain's emotional centers. This is critical. You may not notice it, but your brain is triaging emotional spikes

84

overnight. The amygdala, which governs fight-or-flight responses, is quieted by sufficient REM sleep, allowing for more stable decision-making under pressure the next day.

3. **Synaptic Homeostasis (Clearing Clutter):**
The brain collects massive amounts of data each day. During sleep, it decides what to keep and what to delete. This "downscaling" prevents cognitive overload. A well-rested brain has a cleaned-up inventory — one with less noise and more clarity. Retrieval becomes faster and more accurate.

4. **Motor Skill Enhancement:**
Complex motor sequences (swing changes, release patterns, footwork) are not locked in during reps. They are enhanced during REM sleep when the motor cortex is reactivated. Studies have shown measurable gains in motor performance even without additional practice, provided sleep follows.

5. **Cognitive Flexibility:**
Sleep increases your ability to switch strategies, adapt to context, and reframe problems. These are hallmarks of elite performance. The prefrontal cortex (the executive control center) is restored during deep sleep, improving your ability to make strategic decisions in real time.

6. **Sensory Processing Calibration:**
Your brain fine-tunes how it processes sensory inputs during sleep. Why does the ball look slower or faster on different days? Why do some greens feel "readable" and others not? A portion of this lies in the overnight calibration of visual and kinesthetic feedback loops.

7. **Creativity and Insight Generation:**
During REM, the brain runs simulations. It connects ideas that were unconnected during waking hours. This explains those "aha" moments in the middle of the night or upon waking. Problem-solving is not just boosted but also reorganized.

8. **Reactivation of Practice (Replay Loops):**
Hippocampal neurons replay learning sequences during SWS. If you practiced effectively that day, the brain literally replays your drills, swings, and

decisions. This neural replay is how weak synapses are strengthened and turned into retrievable inventory.

9. **Stress Hormone Regulation (Cortisol Balance):**
   Poor sleep results in elevated cortisol. Elevated cortisol impairs access. It impairs focus. It impairs calm. High cortisol makes your brain believe that the competition is a threat, not an opportunity. Sleep neutralizes this by restoring hormonal balance.

10. **Immune-Brain Communication:**
    You may not associate immunity with performance, but inflammation affects brain fog, joint stiffness, and mood. Deep sleep boosts interleukin production, which supports recovery at both the physical and neural levels.

So, what happens when you don't sleep?

Here are 10 measurable impairments in the next-day performance after even just one night of disrupted or insufficient sleep:

1. **Reduced Tournament Round Function:**
   You can't hold as many variables in your brain. Tactical decision-making suffers. You second guess. You forget why you changed a target mid-swing.

2. **Decreased Reaction Time:**
   Neurons fire slower. This isn't just for sprinters — it affects putting, shot shaping, and even how fast you adjust grip pressure mid-swing/stroke.

3. **Impaired Focus and Attention Span:**
   You find yourself distracted by irrelevant stimuli. A fly. A gallery member's cough. A thought from three days ago. Your brain has less ability to filter noise.

4. **Poor Emotional Regulation:**
   You snap. You dwell. You whine instead of accessing inventory that can help you adjust. One bogey becomes three. The buffer between stimulus and response shrinks dramatically.

5. **Diminished Motor Coordination:**
   The timing of your swing feels off. Your tempo feels rushed or delayed. What felt fluid yesterday feels mechanical today.

6. **Decreased Retrieval of Stored Inventory:**
   You can't access what you practiced. This is the most dangerous consequence. You "worked on that exact stroke" in practice, but now it feels unfamiliar.

7. **Increased Negative Bias:**
   The brain becomes more threat focused. You interpret neutral events as negative. A bad bounce becomes a sign that "today isn't your day."

8. **Poor Risk Assessment:**
   You either play too safely or too aggressively — rarely the optimal strategy. The frontal cortex's risk evaluation mechanism is weakened.

9. **Increased Injury Risk:**
   Joint instability increases. Muscle tension isn't properly relaxed. Sleep-deprived athletes are more prone to tweaks and strains.

10. **Reduced Ability to get to 10 Hz:**
    Sleep-deprived brains operate well above the critical 10 Hz zone. You are too amped or too fatigued. You may hit one or two shots in 10 Hz, but most will be shots you are fully capable of hitting.

From Dr. Walker's book, *Why We Sleep*, here are some troubling statistics to support the above data:

- 4 hours sleep = 70% drop in natural killer cells
- 5 hours of sleep increases heart attack risk by 200%
- 1 week of poor sleep = 60% less antibody response
- Drowsy driving causes 1.2 million crashes annually in U.S.
- Sleep loss boosts cancer risk by 40%, tumors grow faster

When you understand what sleep does for the brain — and what lack of sleep costs — it becomes obvious that performance begins the night before. Not just because you feel tired. But because the neurological infrastructure required for execution was not built. Or worse, it was dismantled overnight.

This is why I now make the claim: **The most important hour of your practice is the hour before sleep.** Not because you are hitting balls, but because you are shaping what the brain will encode that night. You are elevating key inventory to the top of your cognitive shelf. You are preparing your brain to replay, consolidate, and store.

Athletes often ask me how much sleep they need. My answer: It's not just the quantity. It's the architecture. You need enough SWS to move memories out of the hippocampus. You need enough REM to integrate those memories emotionally and procedurally. A full night of sleep includes both. Without both, you are quite literally not the same athlete.

SLEEP NEUROHACK: THE 4-1-1 METHOD

Sleep is not just influenced by how tired you are, it is influenced by what inventory is present at the very top of your mind before you fall asleep. Remember: sleep is not passive. The brain is scanning the last experiences of the day, deciding what to encode, what to delete, and what to rehearse.

This is where a final neurohack comes in — a simple but powerful tool that I now recommend to every athlete I work with.

It is called the **4-1-1**.

It takes less than five minutes and is done while in bed, ideally as the very last mental act before drifting off to sleep. Even more ideal is to do this after watching your encoding videos! The idea is simple: direct your brain to prioritize the storage and encoding of high-value inventory by consciously feeding it what matters.

Here is the 4-1-1 process:

1. **Recall 4 positive experiences from the day (preferably non golf).**
   These can be related to performance, practice, relationships, or even small moments of random positive experiences. The goal is to consciously elevate your final inventory. You're telling your brain: *these are worth keeping*.

2. **Acknowledge 1 negative experience from the day.**
   Do not ignore it. Ignored spikes still encode. By consciously identifying it, you reduce the likelihood of it becoming dominant overnight. You take back control.

3. **Identify 1 simple action for tomorrow that could positively impact the negative experience.**

   This gives your brain a sense of closure. A sense of agency. And perhaps most importantly, it converts a negative loop into a problem-solving loop—which is a dramatically different neural environment.

I have seen remarkable outcomes with athletes who have committed to this 4-1-1 process nightly:

- Increased quality and depth of sleep
- Increased morning cognitive clarity and focus
- Diluted overnight encoding of negative experiences
- Enhanced repair of overused neural circuits (the "roads" that were most taxed during the day)
- A clear, actionable purpose for the following day

I have said throughout this chapter that the hour before sleep is the most important hour of your day. The 4-1-1 neurohack is the final step in protecting that hour. It is not a replacement for mindfulness, meditation, or journaling — but it is a highly practical, neuroscience-backed primer for sleep.

You are giving your brain a final note before it composes an entire overnight symphony of memory and reactivation. What song do you want it to play?

In a world where performance comes down to what inventory is accessible at the right time, what you do in those last five minutes before sleep might matter more than what you did earlier for five hours on the range.

🔑 Key Takeaways

- Sleep is not rest — it is an active neurological process that consolidates memory, regulates emotion, and enhances motor skills.
- Poor sleep disrupts 10 Hz brain states, impairing performance, focus, decision-making, and motor coordination.

- Memory from practice is transferred during deep sleep (SWS) and refined during REM.
- Sleep-deprived athletes struggle with retrieval, risk assessment, and emotional control — despite good preparation.
- The brain encodes top-of-mind inventory; manage what you consume before bed to prioritize performance memory.
- Use the 4-1-1 method: 4 positives, 1 negative, 1 action — this directs the brain's overnight encoding.
- The hour before sleep is the most important of your day — protect it to unlock your best game.

There is an amazing source of knowledge and skills inventory specific for you, available to you in seconds when you compete that has no subscription fees or Wi-Fi needed to access. It's your brain. It only needs to be calm to give you full access.

09 | CASE STUDIES

Coaches Around the World Share

The most impactful golf lesson you can take is learning how to reduce the noise in your head, especially over shots. The dispersion of your shots with a less noisy brain is significantly smaller.

Now that we've explored the strategies and insights of chasing 10 Hz throughout this book, it is time to see them in action. In this chapter, certified coaches from around the world bring the concepts from the previous chapters to life through real-world case studies. Each case study demonstrates the power of having a simpler language (Green, Yellow, Red) and having quick ready-to-go tools of neurohacks. These stories are proof that the principles I have shared (and which you can learn) aren't just ideas — they're catalysts for real success. Let their journeys inspire your own.

CASE STUDY 1: *The Traffic Light to Better Performance*

Coach: Darcy Dhillon
Contact: darcy@ddcoaches.com | www.ddcoaches.com | @ddcoaches

Background:

Over the past two years, I've worked with a 14-year-old female athlete who showed early signs of potential but struggled with maintaining consistent focus during our sessions. She travels over an hour and a half to reach my location, usually arriving after a long car ride with her father. While she often starts off engaged, her concentration quickly declines, especially after unsolicited comments or interruptions from her dad.

Approach:

To help her better understand her internal state and take ownership of her focus, I introduced a "traffic light" framework — Green, Yellow, and Red — to describe her brain's performance potential:

- Green: High performance zone (80% success rate), like cruising down an open highway.
- Yellow: Moderately distracted (40%), like navigating light city traffic.
- Red: Highly distracted and reactive (5%), like stuck in post-game chaos leaving an Edmonton Oilers match.

Using this language, we framed her focus as something observable and manageable. We then introduced three specific neurohacks:

- 10-2 Method (most powerful, reduces surprise)
- Hands 5 (moderate grounding technique)
- 4-2-8 Breathing (light reset, calming)

Together, we practiced each tool, and she began to self-report her color zone during the session. When she felt herself slipping into Yellow or Red, we used the appropriate neurohack in real time. She noticed immediate improvements in her ability to stay present and recalibrate her focus.

Outcome:

By reframing attention as something fluid — but trainable — we gave her control. Her ability to verbalize her state and apply a neurohack deepened her engagement. Sharing this progress with her father also created buy-in on his part and improved the overall training environment.

REFLECTION: Old Me vs. New Me

Old Me:

I might have told her to "just focus more" and doubled down on technique, unknowingly increasing the pressure.

New Me:

I now realize that helping athletes recognize and manage their mental state using tools like neurohacks is far more effective. We all perform better in GREEN — and now she knows how to get there.

CASE STUDY 2: *The Target Shift – Rewiring Visualization for Performance*

Coach: Salimah Mussani
Title: Stollery Family Team Canada Head Coach – Women's

Background:

Working with elite players often reveals gaps that are hidden beneath layers of talent and training. I was introduced to Dr. Izzy Justice through our Canadian National Team network, and within just a few months of integrating his brain-based methodology, we started to uncover — and solve — key neurological blind spots in our players' routines.

One such case was an elite player struggling with consistency on the putting green, particularly on left-to-right putts. Despite high skill and work ethic, she couldn't start the ball on line and repeatedly missed low. While her external routine was inconsistent, my intuition was that her internal targeting system — her visualization and memory recall — was equally underdeveloped.

Approach:

Using GYRA (Get Your Reps Accurate) and Dr. Justice's principles around memory and neural engagement, we decided to break the pattern. I had her hit 10-foot putts of various slopes and introduced different *external* targets for a single left-to-right putt:

1. A tee beside the hole (break line reference)
2. A coin at the apex of the putt
3. A chalk dot one foot in front of the ball (start line)
4. A marker near the hole to indicate where the ball should enter

She made all four putts. The moment was powerful. Her brain was no longer locked into just aiming at the hole — a strategy that doesn't account for slope and often fails under pressure. This opened the door to a larger neurological insight: golf is not a reactive sport like hockey or tennis. We don't see the target while we execute. We must rely on our internal ability to hold a memory of the target.

To prove this point, I asked her to close her eyes and describe her childhood bedroom. Without hesitation, she described it in vivid detail: the wallpaper, furniture, trophies, even the location of her books and stuffed animals. That clarity of recall is the same brain function we need when visualizing a putt.

Outcome:

She realized that visualization in putting is not about repetition, it's about memory. And more importantly, each putt requires a unique target. The brain performs best when engaged dynamically. Her new routine is now centered around one question in the final 10 seconds before execution:

"What FORCE should I apply to get my ball to my end TARGET?"

This neurological anchor not only improves performance, but it also clears the noise.

REFLECTION: Old Me vs. New Me

Old Me:

I might have worked on technical cues or alignment drills, hoping she'd eventually find her rhythm on left-to-right putts.

New Me:

I now coach the *brain* first. By understanding how memory and target selection actually work, we created a repeatable *mental* routine — one that changed everything for her.

CASE STUDY 3: *US Kids World Championship – The Power of Reset*

Coach: Carla Overhiser
Contact: cmwasienko@gmail.com | @carwas17

Background:

At the US Kids World Championship, I was coaching a junior player competing at a very high level. She had played exceptionally well throughout the first two days and entered the final hole of the second round just two shots off the lead. Her tee shot on a drivable par-4 left her just short of the green — an ideal setup to finish strong.

But as she walked toward the green, the pressure changed. A large gallery had formed. Cheers. Noise. Presence. She later shared that the moment she heard the crowd, her brain immediately spiked to Red. She proceeded to skull her chip over the green, chipped again to four feet, and then missed the putt — making double bogey on what could have been an eagle or birdie opportunity. The disappointment was visible.

Approach:

Instead of heading to the range or short game area after the round, I took her to lunch. I intentionally said nothing about the final hole. The goal was not to fix technique, but to reset frequency. Only later, when *she* initiated the conversation, did we revisit the moment.

She identified the shift to Red the second she saw and heard the crowd. She recognized that she had no tool ready to regulate her state in that moment, which affected her ability to focus on her target or feel the appropriate force. This insight was powerful.

Together, we reviewed simple neurohacks that could be deployed under pressure:

- 4-2-8 breathing to calm and reset.
- 10-2 recall to reduce surprise and refocus.

We mentally rehearsed how she might use these tools if the situation repeated.

Outcome:

The very next day, she came back focused, steady, and emotionally regulated. She shot an incredible 4-under in the final round and finished second in the World Championships. The difference wasn't skill — it was state.

REFLECTION: Old Me vs. New Me

Old Me:

After a final-hole double, I would have had her practice chip shots and debrief the round immediately, thinking it was a technical issue.

New Me:

Now I understand that emotional spikes derail performance faster than mechanics ever could. She didn't need practice, she needed recovery. Taking her to lunch instead of talking about golf helped bring her back to Green, and that mental reset was the foundation for her best round of the week.

CASE STUDY 4: *From Red to Green in One Hour*

Coach: Tim Sheredy
Session Type: One-Hour Golf Lesson – Full Swing

Background:

Conlin came to his lesson frustrated with his ball striking. From the moment he began warming up, it was evident his brain was operating in

Red. His body language told the story: one-armed finishes, negative self-talk, and visible emotional escalation after every swing. Recognizing that any mechanical intervention would be ineffective until his state changed, the first objective became clear: get Conlin to Green.

Approach:

To shift him neurologically, I started with an EQ Focal Thought — one customized specifically for him. Conlin is a passionate Georgia Bulldogs fan, and we talked about the team's upcoming game that night, as well as their national championship win the previous year. This personal and emotionally charged conversation lasted 3–5 minutes, just enough to interrupt the negative loop and shift his attention.

Once he was slightly more regulated, I introduced the 10-2 Neurohack, guiding him through the process. After that, I filmed his swing. With his brain now in a calmer, more receptive Green state, we were able to analyze the footage and begin technical adjustments.

To reinforce swing changes while keeping his brain engaged, we used a dynamic drill sequence:

- Ball 1: Pause at the top to feel the new, shorter backswing
- Ball 2: Full motion at 50% speed
- Ball 3: Full swing at full speed

This cycle was repeated with a new club and target every three balls to maintain novelty and cognitive stimulation.

At the end of the session, I showed Conlin his before-and-after video and recorded him verbalizing what his brain needed to store. This deepened the encoding process and gave him ownership over the lesson.

Outcome:

Conlin left the session happy, with clear improvements in his swing and a deeper understanding of how emotional regulation impacts performance. He walked away with three practical tools: the 10-2 Neurohack, an EQ Focal Thought, and breathing exercises. As a coach, I was also pleased—not just with the swing changes, but with how effectively we shifted his brain from chaos to clarity.

REFLECTION: Old Me vs. New Me

Old Me:

I would have gone straight to swing mechanics, trying to force technical change onto a distracted, emotionally elevated brain.

New Me:

I now know that no technical fix works in Red. By getting Conlin to Green first, we laid the foundation for learning, retention, and confidence. The neurohacks didn't just help with the lesson — they transformed it.

CASE STUDY 5: *High Stakes Flop Shot – From Code Red to Complete Control*

Coach: Justin Tang
Contact: justin@elitegolfswing.com | @elitegolfswing

Background:

While teaching a group of junior golfers the technique and feel required for flop shots, I was demonstrating a method that increases the probability and ease of execution — even from tight lies. Shot after shot, I was executing clean, high-arching flops with confidence and consistency. At the height of my demonstration, I casually declared that the technique was so reliable I could pull it off even if two students stood right in front of me.

Without hesitation, two 11-year-olds walked forward and stood a few feet ahead — turning this into a real moment of pressure. To make matters more intense, one of their parents was filming from behind. This was a full-blown Code Red moment.

Approach:

In just a few seconds, I had to recalibrate my internal state. I deployed two tools from the Neuro580 system: The 3Ps and The 3 Eyes.

The 3Ps helped me affirm my confidence:

- I have solid technical skill as a player
- I'm teaching from scientific understanding as a coach
- I'm in rhythm, having executed this shot flawlessly several times already

The 3 Eyes helped me ground into the moment:

- Two kids standing in front of me
- They are 1.5 meters tall — below my normal swing plane
- I locked onto the specific spot on the ground where the club needed to make contact

By combining self-affirmation with visual anchoring, I immediately dropped into Green. I executed the shot perfectly — just like the five before it.

Outcome:

What could have been a disaster turned into a memorable moment of composure and control. There was no physical difference between that shot and the others — only the perceived consequences. By managing state, not swing, I proved both to myself and my students that performance under pressure is a brain game first.

REFLECTION: Old Me vs. New Me

Old Me:

I would have backed off the statement or let fear hijack my swing — likely blading the ball and confirming my worst thoughts.

New Me:

Now I understand that state is everything. Tools like the 3Ps and 3 Eyes gave me access to my best swing, even under real, visible pressure.

CASE STUDY 6: *From Reaction to Regulation*

Coach: Dino Ferrer
Contact: dfgolfcoach@gmail.com | @lasellagolfacademy | www.clasesdegolfcostablanca.com | @dfgolfcoach

Background:

In a group session with my competitive juniors — handicaps ranging from 14 down to +1 — I introduced the fundamentals of GYRA Golf. We explored the Red-Yellow-Green brain states, the concept of mind wandering, how to self-assess mental performance, and practical neurohacks like using the senses and the red/yellow card system. I also encouraged them to use the NEURO580 app to track their mental game in real time.

While the whole group was engaged, one player — Stefans — absorbed the material immediately. His attention was laser-focused during the session. In the following weeks, he competed in a WAGR (World Amateur Golf Ranking) tournament and messaged me to share that he'd used several neurohacks to regulate his state and stay in Green.

Just a year earlier, Stefans had been struggling. A missed putt would trigger emotional outbursts — throwing clubs, slamming equipment — and his handicap had risen from +1 to nearly 3. He had even considered quitting.

But during this WAGR event, Stefans practiced emotional awareness before each shot. He used his senses — focusing on landscapes, trees, and colors — to stay grounded and prevent spiraling. He played with calm, awareness, and control. Not only did he compete well, but he won. The next week, he won again. And in June, he claimed victory at the Spanish Faldo Series event, beating a field of strong players.

In a WhatsApp message exchange, he shared:

"I've been working on implementing this principle into my game and life, and it's very interesting. Speaking in terms of colors, I don't think I have gotten red at any point, and a lot of the stuff you taught us truly helps. So, thanks for that—you should do more mental game sessions."

Outcome:

Stefans transformed from a reactive player to a regulated competitor. The difference was not technique — it was awareness. By learning how to recognize and reset his brain state, he reconnected with performance, and more importantly, with joy in the game.

REFLECTION: Old Me vs. New Me

Old Me:

Might have coached through his anger with technical solutions, focusing on swing adjustments or routines.

New Me:

Now I understand that emotional regulation is the gateway to performance. Helping Stefans go from Red to Green gave him back control, enjoyment, and results.

CASE STUDY 7: *My Neuro Diet Before a Golf Tournament*

Coach: Marina Bobeldijk
Contact: marina.bobeldijjk@icloud.com | Facebook: Marina Bobeldijk

Background:

Peak performance is not random. It's designed. Over time, I've developed a personalized "Neuro Diet" that allows me to enter competition feeling grounded, focused, and fully present. It's a combination of physical routines, mental preparation, and intentional use of neurohacks across the 36 hours surrounding a tournament round.

This case study outlines the structured preparation I follow both the day before and on the day of a tournament, with the goal of entering Green and staying there.

Approach:

The Day Before the Tournament:

- Morning Routine:
  Wake at 6am → 20-minute meditation → 10 minutes of mobility → 1-minute ice cold shower → Breakfast with protein, fruit, nuts, and probiotics.

- On-Course Practice:
  - *Short Game:* "Par 18" challenge on the chipping area, emphasizing target awareness.
  - *Putting:* One-ball routine with focus on holding the target.
  - *Range:* Max 30 balls—each with a different club, flight, and target.
  - *Play 9 holes:* Observe emotional temperature, anticipate possible surprises.

- Evening Routine:
  - Create a Golf Mantra (e.g., gratitude).
  - Write down Commitments for tomorrow (e.g., hold target, observe emotional state, use neurohacks).
  - Plan how to handle surprises (e.g., missed short putt).
  - Dinner at 6pm → Watch a nature or comedy film → No devices after 7pm.
  - 30 minutes of yin yoga → Warm shower → In bed by 9pm.

- Sleep Routine:
  - Visualize playing the course: surroundings, feel, motion.
  - Reflect on 3 things to be grateful for.
  - Use 4-1-1: 4 positives, 1 negative, and 1 solution.
  - Fall asleep to ocean or rainfall sounds → Lights off by 9:30pm.

Tournament Day:

- Repeat morning routine.
- En route to course: listen to energizing playlist.
- Arrive 90 minutes early → No phone.
- Range: Play the course mentally (max 30 balls).
- Chipping: "Par 18" with attention to surroundings and target.
- Putting: Practice putts likely to occur, use neurohacks if missed.

During the Round:

- Monitor emotional temperature, adjust as needed.
- Stick to commitments and Golf Mantra.
- Stay calm, focused, and smile often.
- Accept mistakes, enjoy the moment.

Outcome:

By following this Neuro Diet, I consistently arrive in Green and stay there throughout the competition. It's not about superstition or ritual—it's about designing a neurological environment that supports clarity, adaptability, and joy under pressure.

REFLECTION: Old Me vs. New Me

Old Me:

I used to arrive at tournaments stressed, reactive, and overly focused on results — without a plan to manage my internal state.

New Me:

Now I treat tournament prep like a sacred process. My Neuro Diet creates a consistent mental environment that gives me the best chance to play freely, focused, and happy.

What these stories reveal is powerful: the pursuit of 10 Hz focus is not an abstract goal, but a practical, repeatable skill. Time and again, these coaches and their golfers demonstrated that it is possible to reach a calm, focused state in under a minute, even under the highest pressure or confusion. By getting to Green first, instruction and learning became easier and productive. They reached the green zone — calm, clear, and ready — in less than a minute, showing that with practice, this state is within anyone's reach.

🔑 Key Takeaways

- Real stories bring theory to life, proving that neurohack principles work when put into action.
- Challenges become opportunities when neurohack strategies are applied with purpose and consistency.
- Success is not just about knowledge but about *using* knowledge under real-world pressure.
- Mindset, preparation, and resilience turn ideas into breakthroughs.
- Lessons from these stories serve as practical roadmaps for applying these neurohacking tools in your own journey.

Marcus Aurelius: "The soul becomes dyed with the color of its thoughts."

Dr. Justice: "Thoughts are electricity. We are constantly changing electricity. Manage electricity and you manage your thoughts. Manage your thoughts and you are Master of Your Life Experience."

10 | EPILOGUE

The Lifelong Pursuit of Golf by Jim Hinckley

It is an honor to write the Epilogue to this groundbreaking book. Allow me to offer some context on who I am, and why—at this stage of my life—I'm more passionate than ever about leaving behind a game that can be understood, enjoyed, and passed down for generations to come.

I fell in love with golf the moment I picked up a club at the age of 13. I was drawn to everything about it: the time spent outdoors, the competition, the culture, the camaraderie, the joy, the frustration, and above all, the endless opportunity for lifelong learning. From that moment on, I've been in constant pursuit of becoming better at the game.

I've been fortunate that my career path has afforded me unique opportunities within the world of golf. I began humbly, earning minimum wage at ClubCorp, a Dallas-based company that has since evolved into Invited — the largest owner of golf courses in the United States. From those early beginnings, I worked my way up — first as a golf professional, then at the corporate level, eventually becoming President of ClubCorp. At that time, we operated over 200 clubs, generated more than $1 billion in annual revenue, and employed over 22,000 team members. It was a deeply rewarding chapter in my life, filled with opportunities to work with iconic properties like Pinehurst Resort and Firestone Country Club.

Later, I founded Century Golf Partners and partnered with Arnold Palmer to acquire the Arnold Palmer Golf Management brand. Today, our portfolio includes 65 courses, including legends like PGA West. Over the course of my career, I've been involved in the ownership and management of more than 500 golf courses worldwide. I've built or remodeled over 30 of them, collaborating with some of the most celebrated architects in the game. I've had the privilege of hosting more than 100 PGA, LPGA, and USGA tournaments—including 18 major championships.

Along the way, I've had the chance to play some of the world's greatest courses and forge meaningful relationships with the game's most respected instructors and players. What continues to drive me, above all else, is the desire to improve, especially at golf.

I've spent countless hours learning from world-renowned instructors like Dave Pelz, David Leadbetter, and Chris Como. We've hit balls together, shared lessons, played rounds, and debated swing theory late into the night. I've always immersed myself in the latest research and training techniques.

My office has a TrackMan simulator, and my backyard features a chipping and putting green. I belong to a Top 100 club in Dallas, Texas, and I own nearly every golf training aid ever invented. I practice more than I play, constantly chasing progress.

What has fascinated me most in recent years is the explosion of data and technology that has transformed how we understand and teach the game. Today, we can measure the golf ball, the club, and the body in real time. This research has completely changed how we generate power, consistency, and efficiency in the swing.

And yet, for all this innovation, one area remained a mystery: the mind. We've all heard that golf is 80 to 95 percent mental. Legends like Jack Nicklaus and Tiger Woods are celebrated not only for their physical gifts but for their unparalleled mental toughness. And yet, for decades, our understanding of the mental game was built on anecdotes, theories, and best guesses.

That changed for me when I met Dr. Izzy Justice.

Chris Como introduced me to Izzy, describing him as someone who could measure brainwaves and was doing truly revolutionary work. I was intrigued. Chris invited Izzy to speak at a teaching summit at one of our clubs in Dallas. I attended the session — and was completely captivated. The very next day, I told Izzy, "I want to be one of your clients. Treat me just like you treat your Tour players."

Since then, we've become close. We have weekly calls, text often, play golf together, and he's measured my brain on multiple occasions. In the past year alone, I've learned more about the game than I did in the previous five decades.

As I mentioned earlier, our ability to measure the ball, club, and body has revolutionized how we teach golf. What Izzy has done is bring that same level of scientific precision to the brain.

For the first time in history, we can now measure how the brain performs in real golf situations. With over 18,000 scans, Izzy and his team have uncovered how the brain responds under pressure—and more importantly, how to train it to consistently enter a "flow state," the 10 Hz brainwave frequency where peak performance lives.

When Izzy first measured my brain, he looked at me and said, "You think too much and feel too little." That resonated deeply, given the demands of my career and responsibilities. I dove headfirst into the program outlined in this book. For the first seven months, I didn't allow myself a single swing thought—just the neurohacks and performance triggers he prescribed.

The results were immediate.

My scores dropped. My short game and putting improved dramatically. With continued brainwave tracking, I saw consistent, measurable improvement, especially in my ability to reach a flow state within 15 seconds. Izzy even tested my brain's response to different grip sizes, textures, and materials. The differences were astonishing.

I truly believe his work is revolutionary.

He's already made a meaningful impact on major champions, Olympic athletes, business leaders, and members of the military. I've told Izzy that for most of my life, I was focused on learning how to hit the golf ball. His approach taught me how to truly play the game. Because in the end, it's your brain that hits every shot.

I want the golf world to embrace Izzy's research. I hope every instructor begins incorporating his findings into their teaching. Reaching 10 Hz is far easier—and far more impactful—than perfecting a backswing.

I believe this book, along with his podcast and future research, marks a turning point in our understanding of the mental side of golf. Imagine a world where golfers of all levels can enjoy more success, more fun, and faster rounds—all by training their brain, not just their swing.

I now watch beginners stand over the ball for 20 seconds, paralyzed by swing thoughts, and I know they have no chance. Their mind is in the red. They need help.

Getting golfers to green — mentally — will change everything.

I've even begun applying Izzy's principles to my personal and business life. On one occasion, he monitored my brain activity for an hour while I discussed various topics. He spotted one subject that consistently caused my brain to spike. Together, we developed a plan—and the results were extraordinary.

I'm one of Izzy's biggest fans, and I hope you find this book as eye-opening and inspiring as I did. Embrace his program, share it with others, and help bring this breakthrough to golfers everywhere.

The golf industry needs to hear the good news.

Jim Hinckley
CEO | Century Golf

REFERENCES

Amen, D. G. (2015). *Change Your Brain, Change Your Life.*

American Psychological Association. (2017). *Stress in America: Coping with change.*

Bartsch, M. V., Merkel, C., et al. (2021). Attention expedites target selection by prioritizing the neural processing of distractor features. *Communications Biology*, 4, 814.

Born, J., & Wilhelm, I. (2012). System consolidation of memory during sleep. *Psychological Research*, 76(2), 192–203.

Calabrese, E. J., & Mattson, M. P. (2017). How hormesis influences brain health and resilience. *Trends in Neurosciences*, 40(6), 353–365.

Csikszentmihalyi, M. (1975). *Beyond Boredom and Anxiety: Experiencing Flow in Work and Play.* San Francisco: Jossey-Bass.

Darley, J. M., & Batson, C. D. (1973). "From Jerusalem to Jericho": A study of situational and dispositional variables in helping behavior. *Journal of Personality and Social Psychology*, 27(1), 100–108.

Diekelmann, S., & Born, J. (2010). The memory function of sleep. *Nature Reviews Neuroscience*, 11(2), 114–126.

Frontiers in Neuroergonomics. (2022). High-definition transcranial direct current stimulation and basketball free-throw performance. *Frontiers in Neuroergonomics*, 3, Article 892574.

Gruzelier, J. H. (2014). EEG-neurofeedback for optimising performance. II: Creativity, the performing arts and ecological validity. *Neuroscience & Biobehavioral Reviews*, 44, 142–158.

Hodgkin, A. L., & Huxley, A. F. (1952). A quantitative description of membrane current and its application to conduction and excitation in nerve. *The Journal of Physiology*, 117(4), 500–544.

Kandel, E. R., et al. (2013). *Principles of neural science* (5th ed.). McGraw-Hill.

Killingsworth, M. A., & Gilbert, D. T. (2010). A wandering mind is an unhappy mind. *Science,* 330(6006), 932.

Leopold, D. A., & Logothetis, N. K. (1998). Microsaccades and visual perception. *Trends in Neurosciences*, 21(3), 116–120.

Liu, X., Ramirez, S., et al. (2012). Optogenetic stimulation of a hippocampal engram activates fear memory recall. *Nature*, 484(7394), 381–385.

Loughnane, G. M., Newman, D. P., et al. (2016). Target Selection Signals Influence Perceptual Decisions by Modulating the Onset and Rate of Evidence Accumulation. *Current Biology,* 26(4), 496–502.

Moser, May-Britt & Edvard I. Moser. (2005). Discovery of grid cells in the brain's positioning system. *Nature Neuroscience,* 18, 118–125.

Nature Communications. (2020). Exposure to negative news on social media increases anxiety and depression. *Nature Communications*, 11, Article 1332.

Palucci Vieira, L. H., Carling, C., et al. (2022). Modelling the relationships between EEG signals, movement kinematics and outcome in soccer kicking. *Cognitive Neurodynamics,* 16(6), 1303–1321.

Princeton Theological Seminary. (1973). The Good Samaritan study. Referenced in: Darley, J. M., & Batson, C. D. (1973). From Jerusalem to Jericho: A study of situational and dispositional variables in helping behavior. *Journal of Personality and Social Psychology,* 27(1), 100–108.

Ramón y Cajal, S. (1899). *Texture of the nervous system of man and the vertebrates.* Oxford University Press.

Richards, B. A., & Frankland, P. W. (2017). The persistence and transience of memory. *Neuron,* 94(6), 1071–1084.

Salovey, P., & Mayer, J. D. (1990). Emotional intelligence. *Imagination, Cognition and Personality,* 9(3), 185–211.

ScienceDirect. (2018). *Effects of brain stimulation on cognitive and physical performance.*

Sohaib, Syed. (n.d.). *Activate your creative mind: Harnessing brain waves.* LinkedIn

Stavrakis, S., Hadjis, N. S., et al. (2017). Low-level transcutaneous electrical vagus nerve stimulation reduces the incidence of postoperative atrial fibrillation after cardiac surgery. *Heart Rhythm,* 14(5), 776–781.

Titchener, E. B. (1901). *Experimental Psychology: A Manual of Laboratory Practice.* New York: Macmillan.

Walker, M. (2017). *Why We Sleep: Unlocking the Power of Sleep and Dreams.* New York: Scribner.

Walker, M. P., & Stickgold, R. (2006). Sleep, memory, and plasticity. *Annual Review of Psychology,* 57, 139–166.

Zhang, C., Sun, J., et al. (2022). EEG neurofeedback training improves athletes' cognitive performance by modulating alpha and theta oscillations. *Frontiers in Psychology,* 13, Article 826049.

www.ingramcontent.com/pod-product-compliance
Lightning Source LLC
Chambersburg PA
CBHW070503090426
42735CB00012B/2662